About the Author

Carnegie X, born Marcus Young, grew up in Pine Bluff, Arkansas, where, by the age of thirteen, he fell in love with literature and nature. It was always in his heart to write about life and its beauty and ugliness. It has been many years since the days that Carnegie dreamed of putting pen to paper. His aggressive nature of writing is his mortal attempt to make up for lost time.

Swerve – The Untold Gospel of the Universe

Carnegie X

Swerve – The Untold Gospel of the Universe

Olympia Publishers
London

www.olympiapublishers.com
OLYMPIA PAPERBACK EDITION

Copyright © Carnegie X 2023

The right of Carnegie X to be identified as author of
this work has been asserted in accordance with sections 77 and 78 of
the Copyright, Designs and Patents Act 1988.

All Rights Reserved

No reproduction, copy or transmission of this publication
may be made without written permission.
No paragraph of this publication may be reproduced,
copied or transmitted save with the written permission of the publisher,
or in accordance with the provisions
of the Copyright Act 1956 (as amended).

Any person who commits any unauthorized act in relation to
this publication may be liable to criminal
prosecution and civil claims for damage.

A CIP catalogue record for this title is
available from the British Library.

ISBN: 978-1-80439-578-3

This is a work of fiction.
Names, characters, places and incidents originate from the writer's
imagination. Any resemblance to actual persons, living or dead, is
purely coincidental.

First Published in 2023

Olympia Publishers
Tallis House
2 Tallis Street
London
EC4Y 0AB

Printed in Great Britain

Dedication

This book is dedicated to my mother, Arlene 'Faye' Dolls, who, just a few years ago, taught me a lesson that I struggled in life to grasp: nothing is more potent than a man with a dream firmly held tight. Momma, I love you and know that my grip is firm.

Acknowledgements

Thank you to my wife, Maria, for backing me in the struggle to bring this book to the public. I couldn't have done it without you. Thank you to my brothers, Greg Dolberry and Antwan Mclaurin, who wouldn't let me leave North Carolina until the book was done. And thanks to those who encouraged without speaking and who cheered without a whisper. The blessed take all in stride.

Greeting

I am Wasa Damballa, the first scribe of the Supreme Being known as the AllGod, the God of All, the AllFather in the Kingdom of Heaven, and the ALFAMAK in the Kingdom of the Orishas – may he forever be praised. I was born a half-humanoid of beautiful ebony skin and a half serpent with shimmering white scales that stretch from my gold embroidered waist to my rattling diamond tail. I am blessed with a hundred and one arms and two hundred hands; in figuring that shit out, some of you mortals will need a fucking hand. I am draped from head to toe with precious stones from different planets I have visited, each of considerable quality. I was the first spiritual being born from the AllGod's light before a single star was hung in the grove of the megaverse. And, as I was born in the tremendous void of space known as the Trap, where the megaverse grows like fruit, I was there to witness all doom that befalls mankind to this today. As I am the first serpent, the Father of All snakes, and the first to emerge from the AllGod's light which radiates from his being without thought, I was gifted with much power.

But, I was a spontaneous creation and not of a preliminary design or purpose as the AllFather has made requisite for the shedding and sharing of his power. He has always required heavy contemplation concerning matters of godlings and holy creatures, especially in the beginning. But, over an eternity, he has destroyed the majority of godlings that materialized from him, failing to hide their power.

As I emerged at the beginning of all things, where there was nothing upon nothing, and nothing was abundant, the AllGod granted my existence to serve as scribe, chronicler of his bitchin' ass adventures, and as a holy companion. Thus, I became the first traveler: immortal storytellers that travel the cosmos. So, I was not considered a godling or a spiritual creature of significance by the AllGod. Thus, I was not given a birthright as godlings like Odin, Balaam, or the Orishas or spiritual beasts like:

Shub-Niggurath.

Nevertheless, I was the first from the AllGod's light. I am the one who sees all in any universe that I dwell in. I witnessed and wrote many tales that extend beyond this universe and into the Trap, the great void where the megaverse grows like fruit. I was the first to chronicle the battles between the Heavens, mankind, and the Collective, the source of all evil. And I was the first to transcribe the stories of the Redneck, the original clan of the insurrectionists, dating back to Cain.

All that I will share with you is verifiable information, held within the Ether and maintained by the holy spirit, which is called the AllSpirit, the embodiment of the holy ghost. The Ether is simply the super high-powered spiritual telecommunications highway with a limitless range. Consider the Ether our universe's unlimited data plan that stretches from one side of the universe to the other with speed ten times faster than the speed of light and twice the power of a black hole.

The AllGod made it so that all conscious creatures, whether man, angel, humanoid, or spirit within this universe, could maintain the truth of existence and the one actual reality that he wills. The AllGod made it so that you, a mortal, could access the truth of his magnificence so that your prayers would have a purpose for every season. He made it so that you need no authorization from mankind. The AllGod left the Ether for all to use, and all one would need to access it is the key. The louder, the better the access. Behold! I smoke the God Bush, the Father Strain of the plant you call marijuana that gives me most significant access to the Ether, and if you don't smoke, mortal, you can't come.

The Book of the Crimson Dead

Told by Wasa Damballa

"I have not left mankind unprotected as the fearful would presume and therefore cry out to me like Adam at every effort of evolution, binding progress step by step with pain. But, fear nothing. Every species born in each universe is unique, whether humanoid or spiritual beast, for I have made nothing twice within the Trap where the megaverse grows. I am the megaverse's horticulturist – alpha and omega.

"I have fashioned a weapon in the unique design of every creature and conscious creation. The birds have beaks, talons, and claws. The bears, lions, and many others have teeth and claws, also, thick hides. The amoeba is forever and will never die as a whole. And the tardigrade shall inherit in every universe for they are perfect and praise me perfectly. But man, whose design is especially unique, I gave superior intelligence, consciousness, and even opposable thumbs. The flesh of mankind is the banner carrier of the soul and needs nothing more for survival than the knowledge to praise and understand me, which requires every moment of conscious thought.

"Yet, in the face of the spiritual warfare that eventually threatens every Kingdom, prepared or not, I have given mortals mastery of Dark Alchemy – transmutations powered by the soul – in both the physical and metaphysical world. Just as I have left the brain's capacity unlimited in evolution, I have fashioned each soul with the ability to recreate what I have done using its own energy. I have left the secrets of everlasting energy within the dark art. I have left the science of the cosmos to the race of man. Let it be known in the one universe that contains man that the master of Dark Alchemy is the perfector of the soul's full potential, immortality.

"Know that I give a great fortune to the Spliff-Master, the master of Dark Alchemy, who has fully harnessed the ability of the soul to create from the transformation of what is already made. Those who have great faith in the One Reality I have created shall inherit prominent spiritual power like Solomon, whom I still love to this day. And as I have created the megaverse with Chaos Alchemy – the Alchemy of God – which only I wield, it will always be the Dark Alchemists at the head of my kingdoms of Paradise, for the alchemist is forever close to my heart." – The AllGod, Exodus of the ALFAMAK, 3,091 mortal years ago.

Act One

The Flag Floats in the Heavens

"When and where are all these Redneck souls coming from?" the Advocate whispered curiously to the soul of General Maurice, famed African commander of the Theban Legion who now serves as Divine Guard to the Advocate. They looked upon millions of souls roaming, clustering, and swarming the great Hall of Heaven, all delivered to the Kingdom's doorstep by the Umvuni Ovuthiwe, the Reapers of Death. The souls glowed in various shades of blue, signifying levels of spiritual strength, the only muscles that matter in the metaphysical world.

"Trouble, Warlord," General Maurice replied to the Advocate. "They came from trouble upon a troubled road, and most likely, they are on their way to the disaster which they call home. What I know about their kind is that they are made up of different Jordians (privileged assholes)who wholeheartedly agree that leaping from the kettle into the campfire is best practice. Regardless, living or dead, they'll make the worst type of refugee. And now, these obviously damaged souls migrate to this great house in a manner that bodes ill. You know as well as I that no soul comes to heaven directly from the year the First Life – Life in the flesh – ended, and yet, here arrive these souls dressed in the most modern white trashery I have ever seen. Whatever else this is, AllSavior, it will be accompanied by trouble and heathenism. I'm sure of it."

"General, you weep over weathered wounds," the Advocate replied as he looked upon the masses of souls, appearing tens at a time in Sardis, the reapers coming and going like flashes of silver bolts, escorting the souls of Christians for judgment. "Don't let the ill fortunes of our First Life fall upon the feet of those who have just risen. Do you not remember the day you came into my service? Your armor was silver, black, and red, and upon the breastplate, you bore the crow with the halo and crown, the mark of the Wrath Writer, Carnegie Black. But, as soon as you came into my service and care, I released you from the philosopher's stone and blessed your legion with my Dark Alchemy, the Alchemy of the mortal soul. You were then reborn and clothed in the golden armor of all who serve my ministry. You now bear my seal of lion's head surrounded by nine suns and one Black Star, which signifies my inheritance."

"Yes, Warlord of Warlords, please don't misunderstand," said the General. "And please forgive, but I died a martyr most severely. Yet, my legion and I found ourselves butt-naked in Purgatory and stayed there for five thousand years, clawing and scraping through the black muck, just like the rest of the crabs. I did so, AllSavior, for five thousand years. That is until the Wrath Writer, Carnegie, the Carnivorous, stormed the desolated pit and pulled us out. He barely knew what he was doing in those days. In fact, I would say he didn't. And yet, the son of a Gaetz (bitch) pulled us out anyway

"My Theban legion of 6,666 war-hardened souls gave up the world when we were told of salvation and suffered for Christ. We have sacrificed in every life. We have suffered for the AllGod in every life. What have these wafers suffered? Did Five Bucks run out of coffee or something? With all due respect, Warlord, I must refer to the Book of Drake in this instance: this rift-raft who have shown up in Sardis don't act alike, nor rep' alike. Not like you and I. We died for the same cause: the AllGod's One Reality. He wields it. It is his to command.

"Good or evil is irrelevant. We all play to the AllGod's tune. All the wise run toward this purpose. All the cursed run from it. But look at these red-hatted souls. They already smell of brimstone. I dare to say that if the algorithms of judgment don't swallow them whole, you will allow not one fear-filled or rage-rotted male out of this bunch beyond this point in heaven, and only a quarter of these women will walk through the grand door of heaven. They are directly tied to their fathers, sons, and brothers' deeds. Even with your leniency, as we all have lovingly labeled you the Loophole King, I doubt any of these souls of women will rise beyond the second floor. I feel they are destined for the Confederacy, and I shall feel at ease for the safety of heaven. The kingdom will be better for it."

All who made up the court of judgment, mortal souls, spirits, and angels, were appointed by the AllGod except for Heaven's Mass Choir and the guards of the AllSavior, who you have selected personally. But, the demons, many of them the first of the fallen, were appointed by Mormon Law. Though putrid and foul, the fallen ones are tasked with one goal, which they serve: charge every soul that comes before the Advocate, a sinner unworthy of redemption.

"Now, now, General," the Advocate said smiling. "All us warriors of heaven have regrets about how we lived our First Life. That's part of why it was worth living. It fuels us in our Second Life to defend what we did not have in our first: true peace of mind, the constant touch of the Holy Spirit, which is the Ether, and our eternal heart. But, you suffered in Purgatory, and I know wounds that lasted so long might as well still fester in the soul. Does that not make you more sympathetic to those lost souls who suffer eternally and forever? Those that are lost in all lives."

The General rubbed the allure of his brown, ball head and thought for a moment of the Advocate's words. Then he adjusted his shimmering breastplate, pulled out a curvy pipe that he named Miss Lanthan, loaded it with a wild, pungent weed, and said, "You know, Ninth Born, I am still learning the Christian ways, after all this time. And my neck hurts, something fierce from having to turn the other cheek so often."

The Advocate burst into laughter as he watched the General take a few puffs of his dirt weed, some real basic shit. The General offered Lana to the Advocate, but the Advocate replied in a roundabout way, "In the name of Trinidad James: don't pass that pence (shit) to me!"

General Maurice laughed, puffed, and then continued to speak. "I would just like to know how all these souls from 2021 come to be at Heaven's gates, right here, right now, when souls from 2030 arrived in Sardis over a hundred years ago! Heaven has the keys to the present. Death has the keys to the future, and her reapers have the keys to the past. It is unlikely that the souls of the Caucasians before us are here by accident."

"You make provocative statements, Maurice," the Advocate replied slowly. "But, I do not think that you are wrong."

The General continued speaking with the Advocate as they stood beside each other just before the Thirty-Sixth Chamber of Kings, which housed the thirty-sixth appointed Court of Judgment. They studied the newly arrived souls that materialized before their eyes in an allure – appearance – of the modern age, an unrecognizable era to the Christian Saints of Heaven. Many of the souls manifested before them wearing military gear with varying degrees of dingy red hats and white short-sleeved, colored shirts. Then, they heard a voice that echoed in the distance, growing closer to the court.

"They are the victims of the Requiem Virus," said General Tariq ibn Ziyad as he flew through the grand hall, his robes of black and golden silks flittering in the wind. "And many of these souls are the victims of the victims who suffered from the maddening disease." As he landed, he pointed to the souls of hundreds of schoolchildren, playing and dancing in the fog of Sardis, unaware of their viewers.

"They are many, also," Tariq continued as his cast of Dark Alchemy dispersed around his allure before landing on the jeweled floor. He spoke softer the closer he approached the Advocate's station, hoping not to stir the Demonic Counsel. Tariq squinted as he came, for the sun captured in the rear wall of the Thirty-Sixth Chamber hovered just above the wall's horizon of mountainous trees, never to rise above. The sun beamed over the entire court, and rays broke through the fog of Sardis, beyond its doors, through the astral plane to shine upon Turkey, where the first Paradise upon Earth was established. The living trees – changelings – swayed beneath the sun to the singing of the Mass Choir, whose banister was set higher above all, taller than even the Throne of Judgment. And the trees, the changelings, who were as far from the choir as two peaks of neighboring mountain ranges, swayed and danced to the jubilations of the ensemble. The changelings felt that every song that the Mass Choir of Heaven sang was for their growth.

Behind Tariq, hovering in the atmosphere of Sardis like a swarm of bees, were a thousand Books of Life that Tariq had pulled directly from the souls that roamed about Sardis like blue-glowing zombies with twinkles in their eyes.

"AllSavior, look!" Tariq said as he pointed to the books. He summoned one book to move closer as he, the Advocate, and General Maurice stood before the Advocate's station. The Book of Life belonged to a Soul in Sardis named Bingo Jango Bronson, a descendant of the Neanderthals who settled in Arkansas.

"Look upon Bingo's book," Tariq said. "It has been molested with some form of curse beyond the Requiem Virus. We all know that the virus is a sickness of the mind that heavily affects the privileged, flaked (soft), and spoiled. But, as we also know, that disease is an unavoidable business of the flesh and should not affect the book or his soul. However, the allure or appearance of Bingo's book is not of black leather, like the books or journals of traditional souls. Bingo's Book of Life is white and brittle, with a red stripe running down the middle. And on its spine, it says, 'Child of Samuel.' Thus, Bingo is a descendant of the Neanderthals, the children of Nephilim. And the archangel, Samuel, is their forefather. They are akin to the original insurrectionists."

"Oh, pence!" General Maurice said as he passed Lana to the Advocate. And in the same motion, the Advocate dipped his shoulder as he pushed the pipe of mid-strain back toward Maurice to emphasize how much he didn't want that shit passed in his direction.

Tariq pointed to more of the books and said, "There are hundreds more examples here. Shall I continue?"

"By all means, please, Tariq," the Advocate said.

Tariq summoned more Books of Life out of the thousand or so that floated in the air.

"Look upon these books," he said. "These Books of Life are yellow with a black stripe down the center of the cover. In the center of that stripe is the yellow silhouette of a fly lying on its back. The mark of the fly is the symbol of monstrous greed. And the book's spine reads 'A Proud Child of Beelzebub.' Beelzebub is the Father of all those who break oaths. He is the father of the changelings that disguise themselves as man and pleat their pointed tails down their legs. Thus, these are the book of the mortals akin to Judas, the original Oath Breaker. They are the most seditious and know no forms of faith. Many of the children of Beelzebub are in Sardis now, and they call themselves the 3 percent Spoiled Milkers."

Tariq continued.

"The covers of these books are red, carved out of bone, and smell of brimstone.

"These books have the symbol of the anti-Christ extending down the left side of the cover. Along its spine, it reads, 'Child of Azazel.' They are the children of lies and the lies of children who will seek to destroy the Church of the Advocate upon Earth. They are the descendants of the ones who will chain themselves to ideals that are like boulders and cast themselves in the rising oceans as they proclaim salvation with their final gurgling breath. These are the books of many who follow foolishly behind false flags."

Tariq sighed and cleared his throat while pulling out his own smoking pipe made of African Blackwood. He called it Jam Master J cause that motherfucker smoked 'hard as hell.' Tariq loaded the God Bush into Jam Master's bowl and lit it ablaze by activating the sigil tatted upon his index finger. He took two long puffs and then passed the pipe to the Advocate, which he accepted, demonstrating what was proper and correct to General Maurice. General Maurice waved his hand in submission, and they all laughed.

"Good," Tariq said, "the laughter will serve us well." Tariq continued, "These books of life that I will now bring forth are the most troubling. These books are crimson red, and their covers are limp and soft like reptiles, yet hard and inconsistent like stone. They have a blue 'X' outlined in white that stretches across the entire cover. Within the blue of each book are nine piss-stained stars; believe it or not, these Books of Life moan and speak."

"What do you mean? Speak of what?" General Maurice asked, puzzled, for it has always been in Heaven that the soul was the voice of life, and the Book of Life was the written record for the knowledge of Heaven.

General Tariq puffed Jam Master again and then said, "Eh, mostly of Redneck matters."

At that moment, a Book of Life belonging to the soul of a Texan cowboy named Egor Abbott, whose people's genes were cursed with small dicks and big mouths, began to grow paper-thin lips that looked as sharp as a jagged rock. Lips so thin that if they belonged to a woman, she would have to paint a clown's face around those slivers just to make them pop! And at the book's formation of its mouth, it showed its crooked, yellow teeth, of which it was proud, and began to moan and shake in mid-air.

"Confederates, excuse me, Conservatives won't primary their demons in the flesh. Ohh, no!" Abbott's book laughed. "The shame feels scrumptious to our hungry, thirsty souls. My people constantly need more, for fear of 'less' is too much for a good ol' boy to ignore." Then, Abbott's book began a tirade of screams.

"Woooooo!" the book shouted repeatedly. Suddenly, Abbott's book rattled to a quiet and whispered, "It's disgusting what the left-wing media said about the first responders of Ulvaude, just disgusting. How dare the non-Texans trust their eyes, ears, and common sense logic? Never again shall we let our boys, who wear kevlar vests up to their ears, feel the sting of the citizen jeers. We must protect our officers as if they were babies themselves. The children are expendable if you believe what the abortionists say." The book laughed hysterically, then continued.

"But, in the great state of Texas, we force the births to starve and harden their flesh for a world much worse. The Cracker race is dwindling, and the Earth desperately needs more, for each new soul born to our flesh is a soul already accounted for in the planet's future wars." Abbott's book did not halt at a few mere words. To the dismay of all in the company of the Advocate, the book moaned, screamed, and began again.

"Freeze! Spin! Let loose the Gulf's mighty winds," the book said. "May the hard current of Odin's breath blow upon your homes and freeze your bones to a brittle death. And for all Texans who live till the winter is set, I curse thee with summer energy bills that make you wish for your final rest!" Then the book began to scream again.

"Woo!" Abbott's book screamed.

"What the tuck?" General Maurice said as he stared at Lana, his pipe, which had two well-rounded bowls, wondering if the double dose of the dirt weed, Kaenix, had fucked him up completely.

"Is that book cover up there talking?" General Maurice asked Tariq. But Abbott's book misunderstood him and hastily replied.

"What cover-up? There's no cover-up. My flesh never even heard of Uvalde!" Abbot's book replied while chomping its teeth, which sounded like a wolf with prosthetic dentures. Its teeth wiggled to their own tune as the cursed book spoke.

"I'm not that high, right?" Maurice asked aloud.

"Not from Kaenix – that pence suck. It's adrenaline-pumping, paranoia-inducing garbage," said Tariq, who only smoked the finest Cheba.

"I know," replied Maurice. "But, it gives me the same super-duper advantage that Olympic sprinter, Sha'Carri Richardson, has whenever she runs. This pence makes the soul faster, stronger, and more brilliant than everybody else, dead or alive."

"That woman who runs like a dove flies does not smoke that dirt, and marijuana has never done that for anyone!" the Advocate replied sternly.

"AllLord," Maurice sighed and replied, "it must be confirmed in heaven as it is on Earth that whatever the souls of the Cracker Elite believe must be true. Therefore, if the wafers believe, then we must accept it too." The Advocate shook his head as he continued to stare at the book.

But, as Maurice questioned the sanity of his own being, Abbott's Book of Life continued spewing out every degenerate excuse of his people that he could muster.

"Biden is Brandon and Brandon is Biden!" the book snarled and screamed. "And they're both the puppets of black women. The offspring of every woman belongs to the state, not just the poor. As a Catholic Cracker, Biden should know that. You have abandoned your roots, Biden, or should I say, Brandon, which is your name in secret places!" Then Abbott's book grew quiet and began to whisper.

"Women are Earthly gods in mortal flesh, but just as we have bonded the Savior, Crackerdom must also chain the womb and labor the breasts if the strife of women furthers the state's interest. To state and country, women supply warriors like the mason supplies bricks. The children of the poor are the cogs of tomorrow that grind beneath the manicured lawns and feet of the rich. You send the souls, heaven, and we'll bondage its flesh. It is very much our Texan way to enslave a soul to the very last breath. We are the Confederacy of Hell, and we burn without flame. The conservative Wafery are proud enemies of the planet, woman, and God. Thus, we are prepared to prosper without gain. We who covet the Northern Mexican land will always suffer without pain. We are Texans, and we stand proud before all our great shame."

As Abbott's book continued to shit from its mouth, all Books of Life that bore piss-stained stars gathered around Abbott's book, and one could feel all over Sardis the Caucasian Cocktail of Courage brewing within the great house. Abbott's book spun around, grinning its crooked teeth. Then the cowboy's book started to moan again like a dog with its balls nailed to the floor. The rest of the Confederate-flag-draped books that Tariq had pulled from their souls also began to shit from their mouths, repeating the turds of wisdom that Abbott's book had said.

The Advocate gave Abbott's book a look of righteous contempt and said: "General Maurice, did you know that the rules of my First do not bind my Second Life? I was about love in the First, but even that was misunderstood. However, upon my return, I am a savage, and I'm all about that Slaughter Gang life! Have you heard of what I will do to the rich in my mother's name?"

"Well, that's why I am here, Warlord of Warlords," General Maurice replied as he put one finger in his ear to quiet the screaming of Abbott's book. "I have it on good authority that it will be a blood bath. That's at least what I was promised by my former retainer. But, I tell you what, you tell me from your warmongering lips of your future endeavors, and I'll share Carnegie Black's version of Revelations with you. And you haven't heard real savagery, Slaughter Gang or not, until you've heard the Carnivorous Alchemist's version of the End of time." Then the Theban laughed as his eyes gleamed with the promise of many excellent battles.

"No heart?" the Advocate asked. "That's what he said, right? No heart?" he asked again, almost nodding his head, urging agreement from Maurice. Then a severe look fell upon the Advocate's face as he thought for a moment amidst the screaming book and said, "General Maurice, now I'm curious, and I must know. Am I a bad Gaetz (ass) in this version of your former retainer, the Wrath Writer?"

General Maurice smirked as he reached into his goody bag, revealing a crushing amount of that stank weed he loaded into both sweet barrels of Lana. He took two puffs and replied, "The absolute 'baddest!' Carnegie the Black gives vivid details of how you will string up the generals of each army you defeat by their heels to the cheers and claps of the meek, not Mill. Even Carnegie's choir, which resides in the Tower of Nabu along with his soul, sings of how the AllMighty Advocate, the Ninth Born to the AllGod, will place the heads of many world leaders and royalty high upon pikes outside the walls of Paradise. Even the demons who hear his version are shaken to their core. It is how he generally coerces high-ranking demons of the Confederacy into doing his will."

The Advocate laughed and said, "Interesting. But yes, he's right. I will. I plan on slaughtering every one of those sons of Mitches and the daughters of the rich. Some will dangle from the rafters by their jaw bones like fish."

Maurice laughed loudly and said, "Yes! That's that the pence I'm talking about! The first place we should go to is the nursing homes and catch their souls before they can escape in the Rapture. The algorithms in the Kingdom of Heaven seem indiscriminate, which is really tucked up! Female souls into male bodies, and vice versa. I mean, really, tucked up. So I aspect the

Rapture of being no different. So we must get those rich carlsontuckers (motherfuckers) before they can escape."

"You gonna ride to the end?" the Advocate asked of his Divine Guardian.

The Theban lifted his sickle to his chest and proclaimed, "AllSavior, it is with us as it was to be down with Lord Pac. We're rollin' until the spiritual wheels fall off!"

"Excellent!" replied the AllProphet.

Abbott's book grew aggravated, for it did not get the rise out of the Advocate as it had wished. The book then ceased moaning and screaming. Abbott's shit manual became quiet for a long moment. Then the book smiled its crooked, yellow teeth and began to chant out!

"ERCOT! With the crinkled flesh of my dead limp, and eroding cock, Tuck the citizens! Tuck the innocent. Tuck the whole tucking lot! Tuck 'em till the summer's a boiling dome of heat, flies, and bloated rot! Tuck 'em right in the Gaetz until the bleeding stops!"

Then the choir sang out,

"Ercot! Ercot! Ercot!

$9,000 for every hour of the megawatt.

The consumers foot the bill or they get dropped.

Racketeering is what we hearin' on the block. "

"General Tariq," the Advocate said, "the book speaks. How is this possible?"

"Well, Ninth Born," Tariq said, "that is the troubling part. I have pulled six hundred or so of these books from the souls gathered in Sardis at this moment. I can tell you that the ill vibe these talking books give off is all over Sardis. Governor Musa is, as we speak, befuddled by the occurrence. The ill vibe has captured all his focus, and you know how my former retainer gets when he's focused; Musa is like a dog on a bone. Nevertheless, AllProphet, pay close attention. I will attempt to destroy the book by flame."

Tariq reached into his robe and pulled out a red scarf with text written across its fabric. Tariq reviewed the text printed in Ebonics, the same language Google A.I. articulates, and then held the words in the forefront of his mind as if they were overflowing from his lips. Tariq then threw the scarf at Abbott's Book of Life and then spoke the following words to ignite his cast:

"Juvenile is in the third Ward, Turk is cursed by the Crackers' cage, Tunechi laughs as he sits above the Earth, high upon a throne of ivory, But, B.G. stands in the thirteenth Ward, forever as Noia's living flame.

"Dark Cast No. four: the living magnolia burns four hundred degrees."

The cast was ignited, and the constructs of the universe responded. The scarf which covered the bitchin' book burst into flames. Then the flaming scarf began to circle the book, taking the shape of many slow-spinning magnolias that burned with intense heat with each flame they carried. But Abbott's belligerent book didn't burn. Instead, it laughed and laughed and laughed even more as it span around rapidly, extinguishing the fiery magnolias with each pass. Then the book moved closer to the Advocate as the magnolias smoldered and fell in ashes to where it was face to face with the God Sun.

"You know, Advocate, you are a bastard son," said the bitchin' Book of Abbot. "You, out of all beings, should support the Cracker cause, for you could easily have been rectified if born in our time."

"Provocative," the Advocate said, urging the book to

continue. But General Tariq interrupted as he did not understand the book's purpose and assumed it came to curse the House of Sardis or maybe even the Advocate himself.

"AllLord, I wouldn't," said Tariq. Now, General Tariq, for whom the Rock of Gibraltar is named, was infamous for his quickness. His decisiveness on the active battlefield was legendary. He was the Muslim who brought Muslim sophistication to hillbillyish Spain in the Earth year 711. Upon the horde of Berbers that was his army, Tariq's coming brought science, math, and reading to the barbaric tribes of that land. The people of Spain celebrated the General, for they had no champion but him during that era. And because of his greatness as a warrior and a scholar, he is honored in all spiritual kingdoms.

"These books represent the changelings!" Tariq quickly said. "Every Book of Life marked by that pence-stained flag is not just the descendant of the Neanderthals, the children of Samuel, the first insurrectionist in Heaven. But they are also Children of Cain, the first insurrectionist on Earth. These talking books represent mischief on all planes, for their trickster souls have found a way to create White Phuckery even in death. They are an ill brood and full of contradictions, and I would not fully engage without complete understanding."

"I hear you, Rock," the Advocate jokingly said. "But, let's just say I don't entirely disagree with the Book of Abbott. I would like to understand more to see where our paths are completely uncrossed. Let's say, Book, If I had been born in this era, maybe I would not have survived. Maybe, I would have been aborted. But, there is not a book or Bible on Earth that details the plight of my mother or any mother for that matter. Not really. Nor is there any manual or journal that describes the Alabama (Hell) of a time she had explaining to Joseph the intricacies of how DNA works, which shut the man down for the rest of his days. The last I talked to Joseph, which was just as I started my ministry, he mumbled what he always mumbled; something to the effect of:

"'If only Pepaw Adam was not fearful of the pussy. If only he would have grabbed Memaw Eve by the pussy, like she must have wanted, as all women must want. Maybe we would not be in this predicament of fearing everything a woman says and does.'

"But, also," the Advocate continued, "my actual Father, the AllFather, promised my ancestor Adam that he would return, flesh and blood, in five thousand years, a day to an immortal. Adam, like Joseph, didn't understand, so they both wept like Mitches (bitches) for their reasons. Nevertheless, precisely five thousand years later, to the 'whatever' attitude of Joseph and the dismay of every ruler of that era, the AllGod kept his word. I am his word, and I am, after all these years, like brother Elton over there, still standing."

The Advocate pointed to Elton, who was brought to Heaven early to complete the Mass Choir's instrumental ensemble. Elton winked at the Advocate and immediately addressed the Mass Choir.

"One, and a two, and a three..." Lord Elton said to the band and choir as they readied themselves to perform his much-beloved song, "I'm Standing," but sadly was interrupted by the Advocate, who still had a bone to pick with the Book of Abbott.

"Not now, Elton!" the Advocate said.

"Then why did you bring me to this blasted place? It's gorgeous and all but not really Heaven-Heaven. Well, not the inside, anyway. You know, I was booked until 2035," Lord Elton yelled, slamming the lid to the most exquisite piano ever made by an angel. "Want to get cheeky and have a Tina Tantrum with me, freakin' upstart. The nerve!" Lord Elton mumbled.

"Hey, man," Kurt said as he leaned toward Elton from his stool which was only a few yards away. "You've just got here, dude, but I've been playing with the Mass Choir for centuries, bro, and let me tell you, the solos get old very quickly." Then Kurt puffed on his pipe filled with the God Bush, which heals everything ailing the soul except for the scars that life leaves, and said to Lord Elton, "You'll run out of your own songs very quickly up here. Eventually, we will all be forced to sing 'This Light of Mine,' and no one's looking forward to another year of that pence on repeat. Please, just take my word for it. I've seen it all. I was here first."

"Not now, I said!" the Advocate repeated, lifting his hand to the Mass Choir, stationed before the sunrise that never rose, over a kilometer away. "So, I'm curious, Book, do you think anything short of my father himself could have stopped my coming? Indeed, if you believe that you can control the AllGod's word, which he gave Adam, then surely your people think that abortion could have prevented a Shirley Chism or a Freddie Mercury?"

"Well," the book attempted to say. But like most bigots brash enough to be biased, Abbott's book fell along the razor-sharp edge of words that couldn't be explained away with additional context.

"See, those are colored people that, um, and that guy is gay, so we wouldn't really care... what I'm trying to say..." The book struggled like the bitch that it was.

The Advocate laughed to the point of tears and said, "If all that happens to be true, then an abortion would have certainly stopped the coming of Oprah, who is revered, not in one, but two universes."

Maurice laughed hysterically. Tariq held his face in the palm of his hands in a failed attempt to keep composure. Sir Elton was still pissed about his missed solo opportunity but let out a chuckle when he heard what was said. Most of the Mass Choristers were on the floor as their laughs echoed throughout Sardis. The angels snickered underneath their breaths. Even the soul of John Brown, the revolutionary abolitionist appointed Mortal Guard sentry and the possessor of the only firearm in Heaven, burst into laughter. I mean, the man never laughed in any life except for two occasions: just before he was hung and at that moment when the Advocate put Abbott's book back upon the fucking shelf of proper places.

"Ahhhh, what a time to be alive!" the Advocate said, quoting from the Testament of Drake, rubbing his eyes dry from the laughter. "You've even made John Brown laugh, and I swear that mortal's soul has no funny bone. Book, or your soul, I should say, overthinks the flesh and complicates your responsibility as the stewards of it. The mortals that control mankind's fate's only responsibility is to make the burden lighter, not heavier. I wonder, when would one have time to pray if every man or corporation pretends to play God and overseer? By the way, my father is no one's burden, and he claims that all men are detached from their fathers. It is why the men most lost to the world call out his name as AllFather, the Father of All."

But, yes," the Advocate continued, "your people's population is shrinking, but that is only if you look at it in a small-minded, hateful, low testosterone, Fox News type of way, which is the mandate of the Confederacy, not Christians. There are plenty of ways to preserve and increase your numbers without burdening women and maintaining oneness with Q'Nah Nah Bi'eisha. Q'Nah, or as you fools call her: 'Q,' is the living embodiment of the planet you call Earth, and she is no longer a fan of mankind."

Then the Advocate thought heavily of Earth's physical manifestation, which the immortals called Q, the trickster planet of man. The Advocate was close to Q'Nah Nah in his First Life, for he blessed her with every step he took upon her flesh, which was the soil; her blood was all the waters combined. In return, Q'Nah, fond of the Advocate, honored their kinship and did not attempt to spiritually obstruct his resurrection though having the power to do so. Q'Nah had once refused the AllGod in not accepting Abel's blood upon his murder which was a conflict that resulted in the construction of Heaven, but also the Confederacy of Hell, which is a shitty catch twenty-two.

And as promised to Q'Nah, upon his last departure from Earth, the Advocate made war against man. A war that covered the planet in darkness for a time. A devastating war that set mankind back hundreds of years and killed millions. The Advocate called the culling spirit of smoke and fire he unleashed upon mankind "Dat Nigga 536."

"Now that I think about it," said the Advocate, "maybe you don't call the planet 'Earth' any more. It seems more like your trash bucket. I can no longer tell if you love the planet that was gifted to you, the planet that the Orishas are sworn to protect. So, let me ask you, Book of Abbott, you testament of ill vibes, did I not leave guidance in Georgia upon giant stone tablets concerning population and planet? I even used a racist to carve the Guidestones just so your people would pay closer attention. Q herself rose the stones up from the depths of that land in hopes of a new beginning between mankind and the planet. Why did 'you people' not take heed?"

"You people?" questioned the Book of Abbott, offended. Its yellow-stained teeth, which appeared like dentures made by Crayola, jiggled as it snarled.

"Okay. All right. That's fine, okay," Maurice said to the Advocate, as they both mocked the book. "But maybe Abbott's people feel way too sexy to accept requests?"

"Yes, you people, the Rednecks," the Advocate reiterated. "The ones with that pence-bird flag and contempt for women and planet. From Russia to Florida, you Rednecks are the ones in control, or out of control, depending on how you look at it. But, no matter which eye I use to gaze upon Texas, all I can see is the incredible elemental spirits of the Orishas waging war upon all that lies west of the Gulf of Mexico. The godlings of Africa make war in honor and defense of Q'Nah, the planet, as I once did with 'Dat Nigga, Year 536.' Know that, as you burden others, so do your burdens grow, for the scales of all man's deeds rest in my hands."

"The soul that built the Guidestones of Georgia, that mortal was racist?" interrupted General Tariq, for he was the type of soul whose curiosity got the better.

"Eh, Georgia. Fifty-fifty, at best," the Advocate and Maurice muttered simultaneously.

"How dare you talk about our patriots that way," the book replied. "To call someone racist is to be called racist yourself." All the pence-stains tilted forward in agreement.

"Well, how do you know they are patriots?" asked General Maurice.

"Did you or did you not just say they were racist?" replied the Book of Abbott.

"Well played, jaggles," quipped Maurice, taking a pop shot at the book's teeth for the Alabama (Hell) of it.

The Advocate ignored the Book of Abbott and replied to General Tariq.

"I dare not look into a soul too deeply unless I have no

choice. My father uses demons, goats, bushes, and angels alike to serve his purposes, just as he uses the ants and the wind. So, like my father, I use whomever or whatever without going too far.

"People are freakier than I care to know in this day and age. The pence that the flesh does to the soul is a strange trip that I care not to take."

"Honestly," continued Maurice. "I've never met a stone cutter that wasn't racist. Look at any statue's tiny Hawley (dick) from my era. I mean, some teeny Hawleys. If that's not self-hate, then I don't know what is."

"But, to answer you, Abbott's book," the Advocate said, "Heaven believes your numbers to be acceptable, but if that is not acceptable, then I suggest to your people that they look at the faces of the ones you call African Americans, particularly the light-skinned ones."

The Advocate held his hand to the mist of Sardis and beacon souls to step forward. Thousands of biracial women and youths and White women and Black men with nooses around their necks surrounded the Advocate's station. They were the tortured souls of a forgotten era without color and tolerance for America's most breathtaking "in-betweens." But in Heaven, slavery was a noose designed for two. For every chain or rope attached to the necks of the wronged, there was the tongue of their tormentors, rapists, and would-be masters tied to the other end. It was decreed under Mormon Law that souls who owned slaves of any kind take responsibility for that slave's soul at judgment. And, many Crackers of a wicked age await Judgment in the House of Sardis attached to their slaves by measures of pain, unable to speak or ease the discomfort of their spiritual restraints.

"When you consider all the children your White ancestors fathered and left suffering for generations, there are more than enough of your seeds sprouting all over the place in the modern age. It's a good chance that many Americans of your era are not only the by-product of your self-righteous "right to life" beliefs but proof of your hypocrisy regarding the rights of life when that life is different from yours. Have your people issued the formerly enslaved people their reparations yet? I'm curious."

One by one, the piss-stained Books of Life lined up in columns and rows about the air and appeared like a giant version of their shitbird flag flapping amidst the mist like a wounded duck. The Redneck books shook and turned a darker red and a dirtier blue as they screamed "unfair." And in unison, the books sang aloud a song of their privileged people's rage.

"Brandon! Brandon pretends to be an honest man, But, What do you do when your President is Brandon,

"And he hasn't a plan?

"Joe, wherever you go, we want you to know, that you are Brandon!"

The Advocate laughed at the frustrated books and said, "See, General Tariq. It is simple to dispel all the bigots and sexists, for nothing they say is of deep thought, intellect, or even realistic. Now that Mammon, the Money God, is dead, no godling directs them, which is why they succumbed to the Requiem Virus and COVID before that. So, in the modern era, they are dumbfounded and full of rage; the Requiem Virus did not help matters. But, because they are in a desert dry of wisdom, everything their people say is hypocrisy, an oxymoron like jumbo shrimp or a magistrate that understands civil rights, which is their tucking job to get right. I am disappointed in the police the most."

"Now, who's weathering wounds?" Maurice quipped at the Advocate, for it is a legend in the kingdom of how much the AllSavior dislikes all police except for children advocates and denies all but them Heaven, as much as Mormon Law will allow.

The bitter bitches that were the batch of books fell silent and had been so for some time. Then the Advocate turned about to Abbott's piss-stained book and said, "But, if you care so much about your numbers, tell your people to claim their lost African family. In doing so, they could also enjoy the break from greed that is Juneteenth and the flavor that comes with biracial children. Do that, and your numbers quadruple, and then your people can colonize or gentrify, or however you are whitewashing it these days, a little longer on Q'Nah Nah, or as much as she will allow. Then the Advocate looked upon the floating, talking books and said, "Now, finally! That subject is dead, and we can be forever done with this whine. Someone, go fetch the cheese, for we have all the Crackers we need."

Abbott's book was at a loss for words once again and just floated there, grinding its yellow teeth, mumbling corny negativities about Jews. The allure of Maurice's jaw dropped to the ground. Tariq looked down, smiled, and polished the gold rings upon his hand with the cuff of his robe. But, one of the Mass Choir's tenors, the soul of Andre LaShay Wilks, broke the long silence when he pushed his fellow choir members aside, walked to the front of their stone and gold platform, placed his hand on his left hip, snapped with his right, and said aloud, "Hey, Cracker book! Sit your Gaetz (ass) the tuck (fuck) down! Advocate, we ain't got time for this pence here! As you know, my sexy AllLord, you have until that sun in that wall sets to complete our heavenly choir of a million bad Gaetz souls. Baby, we need some real tune-busters up here, and COVID didn't give us all that we need, though that Redneck virus of the misinformed supplied plenty of superb voices. But, the Requiem Virus didn't give us shit, for it affected mostly the bland, sour, and vocally dry. Now, stop playin' around those Desanti (plural for moron), Advocate! You bought us a little time when you brought Lord Elton up, but still, there's more to do! We need to keep this 'here' moving, honey. Come on, let's work!"

And then the choir sang, "Work, you better work, Mitch."

"We need to give the AllGod some WAP (Worship Admiration and Praise)," said Andre, "and you know how much the AllGod loves that pence!"

The choir and the angels snickered so loudly that the sound could have rivaled a river. King Mirian, and King Constantine of the Council of the Thirty-Sixth Chamber bent over in laughter, for they loved the banter of the Rednecks and the Karens. They loved the craziness of a chubby gay with an attitude, man or woman, with all their souls. And all of Heaven loves the gays and holds them, dear, like babes to mother's milk.

"Andre, it is too early for your sass. Gay it down a notch, will you?" replied the Advocate. "You have all your freedoms up here, so at any time, you can give me a break and stop calling my name aloud," replied the Advocate.

Andre jerked his head and replied, "Well, sweet Advocate, you better take the wheel then!"

"But, yes, book of a broken, twisted soul, Andre's right," the Advocate said as he returned his attention to the chattering Book of Abbott. "Maybe you want to sit your Gaetz down, indeed? Or perhaps, I should destroy you as you so desperately wish?" Then the Advocate rubbed his hands together, vibrating the coins covering each hole in his hand. The air filled with harmonic sounds, lightning crashed throughout the House of Sardis, and it became quiet. Millions of souls lost in the fog crept down to the floor, for fear gripped them at that moment. The book made a puckering face that resembled the star cluster of an asshole and backed away from the Advocate, signifying that it wasn't about that slaughter life, after all. Then Maurice spoke.

"Awww, pence," he said to the books, "you attempt to test us, and now the Advocate has gone electric."

But, as the Advocate charged his hands with energy to lay waste to the yammering books, he was interrupted by Sojourner, Heaven's Command of the Mortal Guard, holy warriors of Heaven.

"No, you won't, Well Spring," said the soul of Sojourner Baumfree, addressing the Advocate with the name only she called him. She stood upon the steps of the second platform that rose from the right side of the Throne of Judgment, the Grand Door to Heaven, which materialized when souls were found worthy, rested between the chair's front legs. When the legion angels discovered that Sojourner was standing on the platform behind them, they broke their attentive positions to turn and look upon such a beautiful mortal warrior and one who had much of the AllGod's grace radiating throughout her soul.

It was well known all over the astral plane that Sojourner's allure was a sight to behold. Known as the Living Truth, she traveled the astral plane for many centuries with the Wrath Breaker, Araminta Ross, upon a golden chariot of fire that AllGod had gifted Araminta, for she was the Black Moses. The allure of dark mahogany-colored skin glowed within the dark blue tent of Sojourner's soul. The age of her face was forever thirty-five, for she was immortal in the Kingdom of Heaven, free to appear as her most authentic self. And so, in her Second Life, she chose to appear "fly" (well dressed) as fuck for all eternity.

Now, the Living Truth stood majestic, covered in blue and beige silk robes that hugged her slender figure down to her boots, both above the knees, where the robe split at many seams and flapped in the breeze of the platform where she stood waiting. Thick links of golden armor covered her neck and waistline. Her allure was that of an athlete tightly shaped, for in each life Sojourner lived, she was a spiritual warrior revered.

"Oh, is that right, Sista Sojo?" the Advocate replied while staring at the Book of Abbott. His eyes gleamed with pillars of fire that swirled around the hourglass-shaped pupil of his eyes. Yes! Obviously, he was pissed off, of course. But as everything ends in a manner fitting his passion, for time is always on his side, he smiled as pillars flared.

Behold! The Advocate slapped his hands together, and lightning struck the Confederate-draped Books of Life and set hundreds on fire! The books screamed with their bitch-asses as their covers lit with flame and halfway burned. They shot across Sardis in all directions, disappearing within the fog in a trail of smoke that smelled of cheap beer and cheaper women. Their screams drowned in the vast House of Sardis, and they weren't seen for a time. But Abbott's book did not move, although being singed. It moaned as its pages flicked flame and smelled of a foul odor. Then the Advocate replied to Sojourner.

"What was that?" the Advocate said. "For a moment, I thought you instructed me to cease. I must have misheard due to the distance." Sojourner sighed and stood at the platform for a moment, for she knew what he would do before he had done it. He often lamented about war to the mortal soldiers and Seraphim angels, about Revelations, and his return as the Warlord of Warlords. It was a daily discussion whenever he smoked God Bush out his pipe, Black Lazarus. So, she knew that most of the books would not survive this encounter with the AllSavior, so she watched and listened more.

"Why would I refuse myself the pleasure of creating confetti out of all these books?" the Advocate whispered to Sojourner, whose words sounded like a sweet melody in her ears. Then the Advocate looked upon the universe which laid in the rafters of Sardis and said aloud, "I feel like Wayne on his skateboard, and I just want to shred some pence.

"Heaven forgive! But, we all heard it from the mouth of Abbott's book and the others. These talking books offer no knowledge to Heaven. They are less valuable than demons and demonic spirits, for they work toward the AllGod's desires. But, these things are lower than those we label the Collective, the source of all evil. Even evil has a purpose as it reveals what true love is; good and proper. But not these things, for they are just White Phuckery in written forms like the tabloids and reek of trickster magic.

"They shall not have a history in Heaven. The future for them shall be paper mache."

Sojourner, not wanting to stir the Advocate's vigor any further, turned back up the steps toward the Chamber of Kings. But, as the Living Truth made her way up the wide, stone and jewel stairway from the second platform, the Advocate turned to look at that ass just as she knew he would, for everyone, including his concubine, Meeka Magdala, knew he liked how Sojourner filled out an Alan Guth robe.

"You are being requested by the convening body of the Thirty-Sixth Chamber of Kings to discuss recent events. And now, also what you have done," Sojourner said while smiling over her shoulder. And as she made her way across the second platform and up the stairs to the Chamber of Kings, she said, "There are important matters that should be discussed, and there is no discussion without you, Warlord of Warlords. Come quickly, please."

What should we do?" asked General Maurice. The Theban then touched the first sigil upon the handle of his long, double-bladed sickle, which commanded the weapon to burst into incendiary flames at both ends. Magnificent was this weapon, for its blades blazed a fire that appeared black, and its smoke was silver, a fire that was gifted by Death herself.

"She knew you were going to destroy those carlsontucking (motherfucking) books," General Maurice said. "But they are not destroyed, so it's all good, Yes? Yes, you burned their spirits badly, but they have wandered off burned but not ruined. The Mitch (Bitch) Gaetz Book of Abbott is right here, which is the only one we should need to spare. The fleeing books do not know they are trapped here as Sardis itself will not allow escape. But, there are plenty more of the bigoted books that lie inside the Redneck souls here, arriving by the cracker barrels at every moment. There also may be others that we can not account for. For a Redneck is not a revelation of flesh but a revealing of the mind and how one will survive in a world set against you. A true Redneck is more than allure or earthly appearance. Being a Redneck is more than flesh deep."

"Yes, brother, praise the Advocate and let him do his will, for his will is good!

"They ain't no Rednecks – you are right about that!" said the soul of a Redneck named Jason Joel, who had the allure of a forty-two-year-old, muscular White man. Jason died fishing along the banks of a lake called Dear Point somewhere along Florida's Redneck Riviera, where he called those waters home. Jason was at the ripe age of ninety when he passed and had made peace with everything and every being in his life very early on.

And upon one sunny summer morning, Jason gripped his heart and starred upon the Umvuni Ovuthlwe as the reaper appeared to him in the allure of his wife long passed. Jason laughed as he wept and threw his reel and his "Salty Life" fishnet hat down to the ground. And with his last words, he expressed himself.

"Thank you, sweet AllLord! Yeah, boy! We did good, and you did right by me. No complaints, no indeed. I have no regrets. I'm dying doin' the thing I love the most. But my soul is tired, and I imagine it's a long way to get to where I'm goin', so let 'er rip! It's been a long time comin', and I've been waiting for this trip."

Jason loved the AllProphet and being a Christian. He was always a repentant soul who told others tales of forgiveness whenever the chance arrived. As a White man who revered his heritage and the story of his people, Jason never forgot the generosity the Native Americans showed to his ancestors long ago. So, as a Florida man, Jason made it a point to speak of the generosity and kindness of the tribes whenever the opportunity came. He was a true Florida Redneck, rooted in culture and tradition.

"Those Rednecks are no Rednecks of mine," Jason continued while holding a goblet of ale. "If these books represent souls that don't love God, country, thy fellow brother who is thy countryman equally, and are human beings who do not revere that beautiful blue marble that we call Earth, then they ain't no Redneck of mine. To Alabama (Hell) with 'em! They're ignorant Gaetz souls who drive Fords and deny their true history. A history of pencing (shitting) on others. Judge them and, if need be, let them perish, books and all. As far as I am concerned, they are no Rednecks of mine."

"Well, Jason, you are spirited today," the Advocate replied, observing Jason's Yemassee attire as he stood behind the

Advocate's station to the right of his party.

"Advocate? The books? The kings?" asked Maurice, eager to fuck some shit up, or at least to avoid being punished by the kings absent a righteous reason. But General Tariq, who had remained silent, motioned to Maurice.

"Have faith and be at peace, General. You'll get used to the pace of Heaven," whispered Tariq. "This is what eternity feels like. It is slow and boring, and then it is fast, and you'll wish the pence would stop, but it's eternity. Enjoy the chill moments. With the Advocate, it's usually nonstop donkey-tuck rodeo shows, all Netflix, no commercials."

"Excuse me for a moment, Jason," said the Advocate as he turned from Jason and faced the Book of Abbott again.

Jason replied, "No problem, Chief."

"No, Maurice," the Advocate said. "I have not forgotten about Abbott's book. We will comply with the request of the kings, for I am like Joe Machin with the options, and they are as frustrated as Democrats."

"Well, that's the problem right there," said Redneck Jason. "For every Democrat, there's a Democratic Chief. And there's a Chief above every hand full of directors in the Democratic Party. And for every Chief of a Chief lies a gremlin who changes the Democratic Party's agenda daily. If there are Democrats up there, then you have bigger problems than talking books. But, I swear to you, my AllLord and AllSavior, the wrong thing to do would be to let my buddy Maurice over here take sickle up there and clear some space. That is the wrong thing to do."

"No, Jason, that's not what I meant," the Advocate said, laughing and shaking his head. "They are kings and only a few Democrats. Still, we've never had an attitude of 'everyone can be saved.' That is a fallacy."

"Because we are Christians, right?" Maurice asked, half serious, half guessing. "Is that the Christian thing to say? Turn the other cheek to get tucked, right?" Jason nodded to Maurice and said,

"That's right, buddy." Jason winked at Maurice, pointed to the Thirty-Sixth Chamber, and slid his hand across his own throat. Maurice laughed.

"But, I assure you," the Advocate said, turning his attention back to Maurice, who craved battle, "we are not done with this matter." Then the Advocate looked intensely at the soiled Book of Abbott and said, "Enjoy your stay in Sardis, Book of Abbott. But I doubt you will be able to fulfill whatever White Phuckery that has brought the soul of Abbott here today. Sweet woo! What great seals of Heaven your people would have to have broken on Earth to generate such trick magic. I can only assume that the trickster planet Q has assisted you somehow. You may regret dealing with her, expecting the odds to favor you. She has sassed the AllGod for fourteen billion years, especially since the coming of man. She has already made fools of your people as the infamous 'Q' on the World Wide Web. What more does she have to prove? Aren't your people burning alive as we speak? Or are they freezing? Who knows with that archaic power grid?"

"It is just 'the net' now. No one says that any more," said Tariq. "How is it that a planet can figure texting and chat out, but Heaven still says these silly things? Forgive me, AllLord, but it is no wonder that your people are still arguing over archaic ideals.

"The Christians are all confused. Forgive me, but I must go pray and be thankful for my people."

"Didn't your people take your head off in Damascus?" asked Maurice, smirking at the concept.

"Testament of HOV," General Tariq replied as he walked a

few feet and then kneeled on the floor. "All who claim or cling to ambition are bound to take a loss, for the greatest successes are built upon the most significant failures. I am General Tariq ibn Ziyad. I am the one who the rock of Gibraltar is named. I am the one, along with my brother, brought great flavor and calamity to the shores of Spain and thus, the world. So, with all my strife and struggle for greatness, I may have lost s significant one in the end."

"Brother, tell me about it. Preach! Decimation was a Mitch (bitch). That's how they got me!"

"The carlsontucking rich!" the Advocate said. They play games with the lives of those they deem lesser. Nevertheless, there is no fear in me. I am like Bone Crusher, giving courage to the fearful and strength to the powerless. I wield time like the potter molds shapeless clay, for everything reforms for my purpose. The true riches of life are seen by these eyes and not theirs."

Then the Advocate turned to the Book of Abbot and said, "You'll know that before the end of this trifle. All shall know this before the end of time. My Paradise on Earth will be established only a day before."

"Oh, I guess you are not such a 'turn the cheek' freak as I was led to believe, Advocate," Abbott's book replied. "But, just go on and ignore my people's plight, the plight of the privileged and perfect. As if you, the AllSavior, don't believe that we are as important as we believe ourselves to be."

"Well, I don't," replied the Advocate. "To tell you the truth, I care about Jews. I love the tuck out of 'em even though I have some bones to pick. But Christians are Christians, and if you are of the faith or follow my teachings, that's that, end of story. You're in. But the buck stops there. If I'm being for real, for real:

I don't love those H.O.s (Holy Offenders)."

At that moment, General Tariq had returned from prayer. "What did I miss?" he asked. "Oh! The Book of Abbott is RonPaulin' from his mouth again? So, I missed nothing. Carry on."

"And you dare honor the Taliban in Heaven? Disgusting!" the Book of Abbott stated while looking at Tariq.

"You people with these names that you can barely pronounce but think you understand," replied General Tariq. "The Taliban. The Al-Qaeda. The Indian guy at the Subway sandwich place, the Iraqi who now owns all the places you love and the Pakistani kid working his way through college at the Bodega – all terrorists and spies.

"Why? Because to you, we all look alike. And by the way, the only thing they have in common is that they are all U.S. funded."

Then General Tariq, in a long-lasting tirade, said, "The AllGod allowed Adam once to name some pence, and you guys just keep the ball rolling. Dyslexic, illiterate, inconsiderate, a stuttering, tripping up the stairs old man, it doesn't matter. I mean, whether in life or death, you just don't give a tuck."

Maurice's jaw dropped to the floor.

"Well, I doubt you will be advocating much without the holy spirit, the Ether, for it is disconnected, and you have neither all your power to speak to the souls of man," the Book of Abbott mused, then gloated. "Heh, maybe you didn't know that? See, we, the Cracker Nation, may be the few and proud, but now we wield that old-timey magic that was lost to my people, taken by Q'Nah for burning her priestesses in 1692, and several other things as well. We've been bad. But, yes. It has taken us Crackers, of varying Wafery, many centuries of drilling Q'Nah's blood and burning her lungs, but now Q'Nah Nah is under our control, and she has released our most wondrous magic, White Phuckery. Trick magic for you 'unsophisticants'."

Then the Book of Abbott laughed and said,

"Q's plight against man is now over. We see everything, for we are no longer blind in one eye."

General Tariq and the Advocate both laid their heads in their hands and sighed as if channeling the great Biden the day Afghanistan fell. Or did it rise? So many things about a mortal's life depend on how you view it. But first, I smoke one, and then I digress.

"What does that mean? What is the book rambling about?" asked General Maurice, his long sickle still ablaze.

The Advocate slid his hand down his face to the length of his beard. "This is about power," the Advocate declared.

"This is about mockery," replied General Tariq.

"This is about gods that should die and stay dead," said Jason.

"It is like the Cranberries have alluded to in so many of their songs. Fear makes dead men of the living," replied the Advocate.

"I shall explain, but not here," the Advocate exclaimed as he rubbed his beard. "We must heed Sojourner's request and cross the threshold that separates the unjudged from the angels who guard the Grand Door and make our way to the Thirty-Sixth Chamber."

"The energy that powers this great house will no longer work in your favor," said the Book of Abbott as it circled in the air, pleased with itself. "I think you understand that now. This temple was one of the first ever erected in Heaven. It was built to mock the ol' God of my people who shared our pain and all of our fathers who fell from Heaven in the days of Cain. Although

Christianity has done its best to neuter the Redneck, we have never given up the old ways, not really. And we shall bring them back with a great feast of energy in honor of a real God of War! Wooo!"

Maurice's eyes lit up as the Book of Abbott teased battle and future conflict. But, as Abbott's book began to hoot and holler like it was fresh out of the squaller, the Advocate touched the coin on the back of his right hand, igniting his Dark Alchemy. Thunder rang out! A bolt of lightning came down from the rafters of Sardis. It struck the book so spectacularly that the impact created a bright light across the great house. And the last thing heard from the Book of Abbott was a bitch-ass, Mitch-ass scream.

"Good riddance," said Redneck Jason. "But Dallas is a fine town. I particularly like the women of El Paso. Talk about some sweet-sass."

"Yes!" rejoiced Maurice. "Now, let us destroy the rest of the books and the souls they belong to, and then let's go to Earth and spank their Cracker families!"

"Provocative, but no," the Advocate said. "It is not that simple. I did not destroy it but sent the book to another part of Sardis. It will be lost for some time, which will buy us more. But now we must go and see the kings and hear their grievances. I'm sure there are many. One king amongst the Thirty-Sixth will have much to say about these Cracker Prophecies."

"Well, Advocate," said Jason as he adjusted his tribal gear. He turned his goblet upside down and tapped the bottom in utter disbelief that it was empty. "This is where I leave you, AllSavior. It is bittersweet. But, as I have drained my ale, I must replenish it with the tribe."

"Is that where you are getting the beer?" General Maurice asked; he had been staring at the wooden goblet for some time.

"You betcha, Maurice," Jason said with that smile that only a "good ol' boy" could give when he knows something that your dumb ass doesn't. "Tribes here have figured out the fermentation process even in the astral plane – ain't pence they can't do. And I know for a fact that it ain't a soul in Heaven who can make a decent brew. All the angels who dabbled in the craft must be Protestant because the Jamaican Heaven has Red Stripe on tap."

"We must visit..." the Advocate and Maurice said simultaneously.

General Tariq just shrugged his shoulders and said, "Keep the beer. Bring me back the ganja."

"Well, um, Jason," Maurice started to say.

But Jason raised his hand and said, "If you have a friend in the Advocate, then you have a friend in me, indeed. I gotcha, playa! The very next time we are near Heaven, I'll bring you a keg. But, that may be a while.

"For many moons, we have been mounted on horses. We have only stopped here to trade. They are taking the mementos of our spiritually dead to Teufel Hunden Woods. The Christian Marines and the Buddhist ROK (Republic of Korea) Marines have taken refuge in those woods, renamed them, and built a small kingdom. I will let them know what has transpired here. Many still feel robbed of their First Life by rich men's wars.

"They would welcome the chance to fight for a worthy cause. And, buddy, no cause is more appropriate than yours."

"Carlsontucking right!" said Maurice.

"Well, go there with my blessing," the Advocate replied to Jason. "But, Jason, I think I need to play this one close to my chest plate, so please, only tell the sergeants if you must. You speak ill of Democrats, but it is the boot officers who I nail to the cross."

"You are preaching to the congress, Advocate," said Jason as he walked off into the mist. "Nevertheless, thy will be done on Earth, as it is in blah blah blah!"

"I like that Advocate Addict," said Maurice as he spent the sickle, removing the black flame that was once ignited.

"We should leave immediately," said Tariq. "But, if I may, Ninth Born, I suggest you leave instructions with Governor Musa so that the judging of souls may reconvene. Your station is technically a formality, as we all know, and the Throne of Judgment, which contains all your father's wisdom, is more than capable in your absence. At least for a while. So, Musa can oversee proceedings with the Chair and the Demon Council, but maybe not tell him about the talking books. He is easily overwhelmed."

"Great Gags! You are right," said the Advocate. "If made aware of the talking books, he would, undoubtedly, overreact with tremendous force, just as the United States regarding Afghanistan. Here in Heaven, we don't have that type of time or resources to waste. No, I will play this close to Urim and Thummim."

"Well, thank goodness it is 2021 on Earth. At least there will be no fist bumping with the true enemy," said General Maurice, who obviously could not tell the future.

"Neither," said the Advocate. "We shall take a long way up, but no worries. We are in good company."

"This is true, AllLord," said General Tariq. "But it doesn't hurt that we have good ganja as well! All praises."

"Amen, my Divine Aide," said the Advocate. "Amen."

Act Two

Standing Orders

As the Advocate and the party, the Divine Aide, General Tariq ibn Ziyad, and the Divine Guard, General Maurice da Saint, prepared for their ascent to the Thirty-Sixth Chamber of Kings, there still was the matter of judging the millions of non-Jewish, Christian souls. After all, it was significant order of business that the Advocate retained as his duty until the days of Revelations.

Now, the generals stood in wait by the stone and gold stairway diagonally left and forward of the Advocate's station. Both generals were uneasy about standing forthright before the kings, even though, on at least two occasions, General Maurice met the AllGod. An incredible honor and horrific predicament that most souls and spirits in the Kingdom of Heaven could not boast of. It was never spiritually sound for a mortal to meet such power. And because General Maurice wishes he could forget, only a few souls in the universe knew that the encounters occurred.

Nevertheless, the kings have often aggravated General Maurice, for he never met a righteous king until he met the AllProphet, the Ninth Born to the AllGod. But General Tariq had other reasons to be perplexed by the kings. It was well known that to stand before the Christian kings is to experience a demoralizing ordeal. So, the generals waited patiently for the Advocate and dared not approach the Thirty-Sixth Chamber alone.

The Advocate had business in the lower House of Sardis, separated from the governing body by an expanding threshold that overlooked the abyss that Sardis was built on. At the center of this threshold, just before the Counselor's stations, is a jeweled pathway that leads to the Grand Door and separates the two Counselor Stations from one another. The Advocate and all of his counsel are positioned on the left side of Sardis before the path. The Demonic Counsel sat on the right, facing the Advocate's station. To the righthand side of the Demon's Station is the swirling pit of fire and brimstone rolling upon itself like lava and hardening like a rock at the top of its twist. As a mortal, you should know that that swirling abyss is the only path from the Kingdom of Heaven that leads to the Confederacy of Hell. Now you may recognize it if you ever should go. Smoke one if you got one!

Immediately beyond the path that separates the stations are two legions of angels, mostly Seraphim, who rest at the ready, for they are sworn to protect the Grand Door from the unworthy. Between the two legions sits the Grand Door in all of its ivory gold and pearls, resting beneath the Throne of Judgment, emitting the most gorgeous light. This most immaculate throne stretches high into the atmosphere of Sardis like a four-legged skyscraper of carved gold, one of many containing the AllGod's wisdom. But higher above the Throne sits the Chamber of Kings, which changes members every three days in Heaven, every fifteen thousand years on Earth. Above the kings sits the Choir who stand above all, for they are the AllGod's favorite part of Heaven. Mortals should know that the best singers are gay, and so many of them are in the Holy Choir singing many dope-fresh songs in honor of the AllGod, for he desires only the best. As the Advocate prepared at his station to give proper instructions to the Divine Aide, Governor Musa Nusayri, he realized that the Demonic Counsel would need to be questioned beforehand. And so, upon seeing the stern look on the Advocate's face, the Holy Choir of the AllGod sang a righteous version of the DJ Unk's classic, "Walk It Out."

"Very funny. At the very least you guys could have performed the remix featuring Andre 3000. His verse is legendary." the Advocate said as he touched his sigil-inscribed thumb to the coin covering the inside of his left hand, activating the Dark Alchemy cast: Ten Toes Deep. A transmutation portal appeared beneath his sandaled feet, where the Advocate sunk, disappearing into the cosmic doorway he created upon the floor.

When he rose from the portal, it was before the enormous Demon Belial, a mighty King of the Confederacy who commands eighty legions of demons and demonic spirits. Clothed in the most exquisite designer wear, Belial stood to the left of his giant throne, which is as large as the Lincoln Monument and positioned to face the Advocate's station. Behind his throne, Belial had placed a million clansmen with meticulous care. They are the collective souls of pedophiles, rapists, murderers, serial killers, and the most honest of general contractors who had earned in death all that they strived for in life. Yes, a retirement fitting of the filth that they were. And they were organized in columns and rows, bent upon their knees like commonplace tricks and hos, who moaned, chanted, and groaned in constant agony, for their spines were fused and chained together. At one end of their unified chains were giant boulders that hung and swung from the right side of Sardis, which was absent a wall. Instead, there was an extensive ledge overlooking the oblivion that is the nothingness of the astral plane.

The clansmen dared not move, for they were pulled by one end of the chains to the edge of Sardis by the boulders whose suspension depended solely on the strength of their unified souls. But, the other end of the chains was held by Belial, who tugged upon the souls every so often. For their love of hate, the hooded men, wrapped in designer drapes that sparkled like glitter, were cursed to live out eternity as they lived the First Life: upon their knees, fearing a God they did not understand.

Belial, well known for his vast collection of Kiton cashmere suits, is counted as one of the Morning Star's lieutenants, for he was among Lucifer's Sparrow Brigade, who sought to murder Cain while the boy was still a child. And after Belial's fall from grace, he was punished just the same as the rest, to suffer forever in the Confederacy. But Belial is nothing if not cunning; as such, he's a sweet-talking motherfucker who charmed his way back into Heaven's gates. And by his excellent knowledge of Mormon Law, Belial was reappointed to the House of Sardis to represent the Confederacy's interest in judgment, for Hell holds the deed to every wicked soul tightly.

"What is it, Ninth Born?" said Belial. "Who do you come to barter for this time? Come to twist my arm or threaten me with dismissal back to Hell? This post is only for three days, and there's no reason to get worked up about whatever you are about to say. You can keep all the blasted souls you want. I give a damn about it. From the pits to the most immaculate palace, Hell is filled with many. We couldn't torture everyone if we tried, and we do. So, there is no argument here."

"That's very kind of you, Belial," said the Advocate as he stared at the massive demon who leaned down upon the corner of his throne. Belial was dark-skinned and had hair of jet black braids intertwined with gold and silver, just like most Seraphim who made up the brood of the Archangels, the Archangels Samuel and Lucifer being the exception. For reasons known only to the AllGod, he made those heathen two pale as a neutron star.

"But you know that I am the Loophole King, and there is not a soul that you can keep from me if I desire him or her to be placed in Heaven. So do not waste your powers of manipulation on me. Your persuasion only serves one purpose in the House of Sardis, and that is deceit."

"Pelosipence (Bullshit)!" said the Demon Rudy Dolomitus Trillianus, the Wicked Bone, a Duke of the Confederacy who was once a human soul. "You carlsontuckin' rat soup eatin', cheap wine makin', son of Crazy Joe," Wicked Bone said as he adjusted his pimp hat and the sleeves on his Eddie Munster-like suit with an Angus Young type of flare to it.

"You know very well the things you do, which I hate. Heaven hogs the pawgs and all the Nubian sinners with them big ol' bouncing Gaetz." Then the Wicked Bone stared at the soul of Catherine Donaway, who leaped from a building in 2002, a year after the so-called "dot.com" bubble burst.

"That Cracker right there!," Rudy said as he pointed to Catherine.

"Cathy, is that you? Oh, yeah! See. This is what I'm talking about! Do you know that Mitch made $115K a year, and still, she sucked Howley on her lunch breaks? That's a carlsontuckin' hustler if ever I've seen one. We need winners and sinners like that down in the pit. Come on now, Jew: shoot the Confederacy a fair one? The Mitches and Honey Grahams (super sluts) in this piece ain't Proverbs 31 women. Well, not all of them."

The Advocate sighed and said, "Although I have a bone to pick with you, Catherine, I forgive you for the burdens your mother bore as an abuse woman. A little girl should not see such things. The mental scars we collect in life is like any other affliction of the mind that runs as deep as the soul and can feel like the AllGod's wrath. But, it is not. The AllGod made us strong and even when afflicted, it shall have us only for a season. Your spiritual scars shall not follow you into Heaven. Considering all events, Cathy, you lived well enough. Go be with your mother."

The Advocate motioned the woman to the Grand Door. Like a bolt, Catherine burst into a sprint so fast that she tripped upon herself repeatedly like Brandon whenever he boarded flights. With tears in her eyes, she screamed as she gained momentum and leaped past the Advocate and the demons at full speed. And as she approached the Grand Door that was barely ajar, she dove in, calling her mother's name.

"That's some Pelosipence to the highest degree," Wicked Bone exclaimed. "You keepin' all these Mitches for yourself, is that right?" asked the demon. Rudy then pulled his glasses out of his robe and said:

"I'll have you know, Super Hebrew, that I've done a little investigating since the last time we spoke on this matter, and it should be no surprise to you that the numbers are off! That's right, carlsontucker! I got the tucking numbers right here, and it doesn't look suitable for the rule of Mormon Law in Heaven if you are letting the sinful women in left and right. There is a conspiracy with the amount of Gaetz in this place. And you are violating the natural order of things." The AllProphet laid his face upon his hand like Brandon, for he tired considerably of the same arguments presented by the Confederacy.

"Piason, Ninth Born, HOVA," said the demon, Wicked Bone, "how tha' Alabama (Hell) are we supposed to entice the souls of the White, wicked and wasteful to the Confederacy if Heaven keeps all the Grahams for yourselves? The wicked souls of men do things for two reasons: money and women. Now that Mammon is dead and that the curse of social media is strong, all we have now are the Grahams who crave attention more than love and money and the Mitches who love wickedness more than righteousness. It is a perfect time for us upon Earth and we should be receiving way more women to torture and control. So, come on now, carlsontucker! Give up them' big ol' butts cause sloth and pride are still sins the last time I check."

Rudy Dolomitus Trillianus lived his First Life as a cunning soul filled with rage and anger, for he did not understand the plight of his people. But Rudy did have a great understanding of the sinful disposition of man. He saw the great humor and irony of the struggle for salvation. A wasteful endeavor, Trillianus called it. But, Rudy understood the disposition of man, mainly the African, so much that he became a comedian, for he found that laughter was a key of Solomon little known. Trillianus discovered that comedy could open doors to the souls of men, rarely used by mortals.

Rudy, who performed under the name Wicked Bone, became the youngest and most successful comedian to emerge from the slave state of Arkansas. He became the first Black-Italian comedian to perform successfully on the Chitlin' Circuit. If you have never heard of the Chitlin' Circuit, imagine a Black Broadway, but with ten times the fuck yous and drastically fewer accolades. Think of pool halls whose tables lean to one side or another. Think of a hot temperature hole in the wall filled with the thickest dames dancing in the arms of handsome hard dick brothers – Now you have it! Sadly, those places don't pay shit, and it's for a good reason.

It is well known in the spiritual realms that Black promoters are not African but shapeshifters descended from the godling

Mammon. They are changelings, crossroad demons that escaped Hell before it was sealed to scrape away a dollar at a time from the souls of the gifted. The flesh they typically masquerade in is always a descendant of the first cursed, a child of Judas. But Rudy didn't know that shit! And as Wicked Bone became more frustrated with entertaining Black faces due to the changelings, he began to despise the color of his skin and all the problems that come from within life in a Black community.

By age twenty-two, Rudy had decided that the Black plight was bullshit, and he dared to dream of being the one percent of America. So, one day he registered as a Republican, and that night, he was visited by the Demon Belial, who promised him wealth, power, and the throne room of many castles if only he would sell Belial his soul. And so Rudy did.

Immediately after selling his soul to Belial, Wicked Bone decided to return to school, and so he began journeying through many higher learning institutions that were unlocked by the demon. Rudy received his B.S. from the Grift University of New York, an M.S. from Yale, and a Doctorate in Law from Harvard, which has always offered free tuition to the privileged demons of the Confederacy. After receiving a New York license to practice Law, which is like receiving a certificate to carpet bag, Wicked Bone successfully ran for Mayor and then Senator of the rat-eat-shark state of New York and won every throne as agreed upon with Belial. But, once Rudy sold his soul to reach levels so high in America, he became enslaved to the Confederacy. And ever since he died in 2020 in the back alley of a Philadelphia adult book store, Wicked Bone's soul has served the Confederacy's interests in the House of Sardis.

"On my father!" replied the Advocate, "it's the same argument, over and over, with you, Rudy. When wicked things concern themselves over women's well-being, they intend to do evil to her flesh. You ask for the Ground Godlings as if they were take-out from Door Dash. In this house, each soul stands up for its own actions unless that soul was a slave of some type in life. This is a nonstarter with me, Wicked Bone. I would not send a true godling of the Earth to Hell if it's not absolutely righteous to do so."

At that moment in eternity, Dolomitus grew angry, and the black curl activator he was famous for in life dripped down the side of his face like liquid brimstone. Then Wicked Bone replied:

"That is that pence I'm talking about, Ninth Born. It is precisely the carlsontucking conspiracy I'm referring to. You have all the Mitches and Grahams in your heavenly possession. And I know it to be in your Jew nature to covet everything, so I have no tuckin' doubt that it is a million Instagram-worthy baes in that tiny Gaetz studio apartment that you call a mansion. Who you try to be, huh? You think you the holy Wilt Chamberlain? Or do you think you are King Martin up there in the Thirty-Sixth, above the AllGod's Throne, having his Carrettas and eating them too? There is a conspiracy of the highest order goin' on up here, and I'm going to get to the carlsontucking bottom of it!"

The Advocate stroked his beard and thought for a moment as he stared at the black activator that dripped down Rudy's face. He smirked as he reached into his burgundy and beige Alan Roth robe, along the lower collar, and retrieved his smoking pipe, Black Lazarus.

"I tell you what," the AllSavior said as he loaded his pipe with the God Bush, Father Strain. "If you agree to refrain from protesting those souls that I am about to condemn to the Confederacy. I also ask that you do not protest the souls I will keep here in Sardis, even though they should also be condemned.

If you agree, I will give the Confederacy of Hell the greatest of women sinners; the souls that do way too much and are filled with the crazy sauce."

"Awwww, Hero, the Jew Negro!" Wicked Bone responded. "This is a deceit of the highest caliber! Do you mean to give us the Mega Karens? The ones we called 'Kellys' in the pits of Hell? Nigga, listen. Hell doesn't want them flat Gaetz, big-boned, loud-mouth Neanderthals in our kingdom? Carlsontucker! Don't you think we got enough of those straw-haired, every perm is a hairdresser's nightmare, shed on the rug wildebeests in the Confederacy? Nigga, we don't want Kellys! We don't wish for Kelly Lynns, Kelly Anns, or even Conways. You can keep your Burning Ambers in Heaven, for we haven't the strength to contend with high functioning crazy.

"I beg you, Super Jew, please do not burden us with the Mega Karen. Don't you think we have suffered enough? Since the '80s, Hell has dabbled in Big Pharma, and as Heaven knows, we made a mess of health care across the tuckin' world. We manufactured the mental health crisis in America in the hopes of filling our ranks. But, now, even the sacred places suffer."

"Okay. Okay. Okay," the Advocate replied. "For real – for real, I will condemn to the Confederacy of Hell the Karens that are a step below the Kellys. You know of who I speak. The White women with the fat Gaetz. The creamy vanilla shakes who should be on meds but are probably not because of American healthcare's poor state. They are the Wafer women too insecure about being with another Wafer, so they settle for Black men with big Howleys who they falsely believe they can control."

"You mean, crazy pussy, that is not technically crazy due to lack of diagnoses?" Wicked Bone excitedly asked. "You mean the dirty Mitches that threaten to call the cops on a Nigga, which is their spouse, whenever a Nigga acts up?" Wicked Bone replied. "Well, all right then, Jew Negro, that's all you had to say. We love those Mitches in Hell."

"But also," said the Advocate. "I ask that you share nothing with Governor Musa about the talking books."

"Nah, Nigga, Nah," said Wicked Bone as he flicked his pimp hat to the side while adjusting his shoulders like a gangsta. "You ask for too much and give too little. If I learned anything while serving as New York's top cop, you don't accept any pleas unless the Perp sweetens the pot considerably. What else would you like to put on the table?"

"Well then, demon," Ninth Born said, frustrated and out of patience. He rose his hand and pointed to the universe that exists in the high rafters of Sardis. "I offer you this. Look upon the universe in the rafters. Do you see the two Seraphim who man those cannons that soar above us? If you do not do what I ask, I will have them fire those space lasers upon you and destroy you utterly and forever. I have no more time to waste."

As Trillianus fell to the jeweled floor and shielded his face from the sky, a voice rang out from Belial's Throne.

"Just give the Jew what he wants," said Ronny DeNagaer, former President of the United States and, even in death, a faithful friend to the People's Republic of China. "The Confederacy postures and boasts of independence from Heaven, but we are enthralled to the kingdom like America is to Saudi Arabia or the world to Russia. If we are ever to be free from the tyranny of Heaven, we must assist the Son of Crazy Joe as much as possible. We are labeled cowards in all the Heavens and secret places. We are the Crackerish cursed that will always thirst, for our burden is the fear of the glass becoming empty, no matter how much it overflows.

"The only cure for this calamity of the mind and heart is wholeheartedly opening our arms and embracing the end of time. You can not contend with the AllGod nor his mortal son. Nor can we correct our course for our ships incorrectly navigate the straights of the righteous; thus, we are completely lost without the AllGod's grace. Just give the Jew what he wants, for he is the master of luck and high tides. Let us proud Crackers not be deluged beneath his consistent rise."

Now, Ronny DeNagaer did become President of the U.S. in the same manner that most Republicans become President: he signed a deal with the King of the Crossroad Demons and Cornerstore Hustlers, the fallen angel Belial. But, Belial did not act alone, for he had not the authority. It seems in America, no matter what type of Manchurian miracle places a Republican in the highest office of the land, his rise is always lent a hand by the preceding bleeding heart Democrat who painstakingly takes money out of the greedy paws of the rich. And in America, whenever a Democratic holds the world's hand in a singalong by candlelight, the Wafery Republic wholeheartedly agrees with Chief Keef when he says, "That's that shit I don't like."

But, for a brief time, the Cracker Nation was not as violentish as they are today.

Rather than show uncontrollable rage or shoot up a school to show their dismay, the mortal Wafer was more sensible and would go to the voting booth to elect their hate. So, in 1981, the Whites elected an actor, a trainer of monkeys, to lead America's zoo-like mob of proud Whites into China's golden lands, where America's trash is recycled and sold back to the White man.

Yes. DeNagaer was crowned King by Belial, the kingmaker, per his deal with the Crossroads demon. Through DeNagaer, Belial gave rise to the seven-headed beast called Big Pharma and, thus, began the siphoning of wealth from millions of African Americans to the pockets of the one percent. Ronny was rewarded for his assault upon the disenfranchised by the Confederacy and given authority in Hell. For the rest of eternity, DeNagaer, the Monkey's King, rests in the Throne of Belial, silent as he bears witness to the judgment of souls.

"Very well then," Wicked Bone said as he dusted his Eddie off and placed his black and white crushed velvet hat back atop his head. "DeNagaer, you monkey trainer trained by monkeys – son of a Mitch. Your Gaetz was told to shut the tuck up while in Sardis, carlsontucker. It is clear to every demon, angel, and soul of man that you are the reason why all the Gaetz we receive in Hell are crazy in the first place. Big Pharma was the beast that grew out of your soul like a tumor upon America and was your monster to control."

"Sure, blame me. Everyone else does," responded DeNagaer. "So many schemes of greed originated out of the '80s, I know. But, Wicked Bone, my beast, Big Pharma, is alive and well and consuming all that dwells upon a planet of death and destruction. To this day, I am celebrated in all the dungeons of perdition, for even the Confederacy has its heroes."

"I assure you, demon spirit," said the Advocate, "the Confederacy has the strongest of the low, which is weaker than an infant if that infant knows my name. I will make waste of you all."

"You are just going to keep ignoring the golden strings, aren't you?" asked Belial. "I know you see these tucking strings I've tied upon to the appendages of this President here – look at this pence? I got this carlsontucker lookin' like Lamb Chop and you straight face? You must of caught this puppet act back in the '80s. Why so Catholic?"

The entire time that DeNagaer waxed solemnly, Belial's hand was raised above DeNagaer, controlling his strings, making the President jump up and down and dance upon the giant throne as if he was an expensive production of Sesame Street's children's show. At one point, Belial made DeNagaer Floss.

"I am pressed for time," the Advocate replied as he placed one hand in the elbow crease of his arm while he puffed the vibrant ganja God Bush from his pipe, his eyes deadlocked upon the jewel floor. Belial stared at the Advocate for a moment, bewildered by the Advocate's meaning, until he looked across Sardis to the top of the AllGod's Throne. Sojourner and King Malcolm were at the edge of the Thirty-Sixth's platform, staring at the Advocate.

"Oh, pence! They are sweating you like its Revelations," said Belial. "Relax about the talking books. I have been authorized by Catholic Law as we have adopted the system in Hell now, to tell you to do what you must with the insurrectionists."

"This White Phuckery is not Hell's doing?" asked the Advocate. "I find that hard to believe. Many seals have been broken and all by the Republicans who are well known as children of the Confederacy."

"We don't claim those tucking kids!" Belial growled. Belial rolled his eyes out of frustration and yanked on the chains he gripped tightly in his left hand.

"Oh, I wish I was in the land of cotton," screamed and moaned the clansmen in unison.

"Do you, my sweet agents of change?" rhetorically asked Belial. "Scream what I love to hear!" Belial asked the chained men as he yanked the chain three times.

"The Second Amendment protects an individual's right to

possess a firearm unconnected with service in a militia."

"And?" asked the Demon King as he yanked another three times upon the chains.

"And the Second Amendment applies to the use of that arm for traditionally lawful purposes, such as self-defense within the home."

"And not what, you two?" Belial asked the souls of two clansmen linked in the back of the formation, struggling not to be pulled off Sardis's edge into oblivion. With deep remorse, the two men – a father and his son – moaned in unison:

"The Second Amendment should not be used as an excuse to exercise evil, and doing so is a disrespectful and intentional abuse of the U.S. Constitution which destroys the power that the document contains."

Belial sighed and said: "I feel better now. I am put more at ease."

"Listen," Belial replied as fumes of sulfuric ash and brimstone escaped his head. Then the demon grew spiraled horns that hung the skulls of cowardly and complicit, and his face took the allure of a Kuda Bull.

"I don't give a tuck what the spines of those books say," Belial said. "Nor do I care what streams south of their pencing mouths. None of the original Satans, who tumbled with the First Fallen, claim these wild children. They are insurrectionists to their compromised hearts, Ninth Born! They might as well be Lucifer's brat who is down in the dungeon and showing no restraint. Hell doesn't need more dysfunction chiefs. We are not the Democrats who dream fruitlessly of a better tomorrow while a Joe Mansion is pencing in the punch bowl of prosperity. Once, we were disillusioned too. We angels, who are mighty and contain the cosmos within our skin and armor, thought we could contend with the will of Heaven and still keep the AllGod's love. We have suffered and are no longer foolish."

Then Belial jiggled the chain in his left hand and asked the clansmen, "What did we learn from the Book of Waka Flaka Flame?" And like a pound of puppies whose tails were caught in the bear traps, the clansmen's pain caught rhythm with the stinging of the chains, and on the beat of rattle, they replied:

"If Heaven catches you slippin', Hell will have you grippin' the ankles, yellin', Devils, devils, devils get off me!"

Belial looked down upon the Advocate and said: "It is these little pleasures that get me through these trying times." Then Belial resumed fiddling with President DeNagaer, dangling him upon the seat and dragging him back and forth like a race car.

The Advocate looked up at President DeNagaer and said, "Look at you DeNagaer. I wonder now that Mammon is dead and the U.S. dollar dwindles to nothingness, do you still feel that trickledown economics work? Watching you dangle there like a DeSantis supporter in desperate need of real leadership, comforts me, for it appears that Karma has summed you up nicely. But, as you trickle down from your strings, I am burdened to think of all the children of your followers and the children of their children, huddled up in one home on a thirty-year mortgage that will sooner be rubble than paid off. Nothing trickles down, monkey trainer, when it comes to wealth. It just causes the pence to collect at your feet, causing your children and your children's children to cling and crawl up your legs from the muck."

Belial laughed.

"You know," continued Belial, returning to his angelic allure. "Most of us are literally burning time until the end of days. That pence can't come fast enough. Hell was founded on the same principles that the mortal's Confederacy was built upon. So, at the beginning of Hell, it seemed fitting that we duplicated the system of the Redneck Republic that sent us so many delicious souls. So many beautiful Marines, reincarnated from the warriors of old. So many killing machines, shiny and bold. It was a golden time for Hell. But, so many General Lees and Rush Limbaughs later, and you are over it. You are sick of the dysfunction, the rhetoric. You grow tired of the coups that happen every day like it's a part of the six-course meal. Do you think we want some dumb Gaetz insurrectionists who will tuck up a free lunch well before breakfast?"

Then Belial flicked the golden strings from his hand and sent the President flying into a corner of the throne. The Cornerstore Hustler then leaned down to the Advocate, looked him flaming eye to eye, and said: "We know not what new games Q is playing with the raging mortals' minds, but whatever it is, it is more than Hell would like to contend with. We will keep all the Jew secrets you want, just destroy the bastards when you are done. Let not one enter the gates of Hell nor climb upon its brimstone walls. Let not even one be a Skogarmaor upon the astral plane. These are Odin's folk, and they are no Rednecks that I claim."

"Yeah, I was just trying to get somethin' out cha', Chief! You could have just 'turn the other cheek' about the pence!" claimed Wicked Bone. "But you are a shrewd negotiator, half-breed. And I guess it's true, you can't pinch a penny out a Jew." Then Rudy laughed and said, "Who do you think you are? Samuel Jackson?"

"Wicked Bone," the Advocate replied as he had caught the holy spirit of the Jonez. "It's all in the blood, Playa! But, either side of your people wouldn't accept a fair deal unless it came with three gold chains, a free meal, and spinning rims. You know, Rudy, you can miss me with that Pelosipence. But, like the Elder Solomon displayed his wisdom before all, I shall let you witness firsthand how the Jew deals fair."

At that moment, Governor Musa came running out of the main body of Sardis, as frantic as a Junior Senator from Missouri.

"Ninth Born, Ninth Born," cried Governor Musa, who came to Belial's station. The Governor had been in the middle section of Sardis and was growing concerned as overwhelmingly rambunctious souls gathered in that great Hall by the masses. "AllLord, I was meeting and greeting in the midsection of Sardis, which you know is something that I love to do, when I experienced the strangest thing.

"I was walking through the fog surrounding the souls near the right section, the portion that overlooks oblivion like the black sea, motionless below a balcony window. Then suddenly, I heard your lightning crashing around me like a mighty crescendo.

"Then, some soldiers, some doughboys from the First World War of Mammon, accosted me in the darkness, and then they chased me to the midsection of Sardis."

"Musa, are you okay? Are you okay, Musa?" asked the Advocate with great concern.

"My liege," Governor Musa continued, too distraught to acknowledge the Advocate's concern. "I was accosted, and they chased me to the midsection of Sardis. And I was struck. I was struck dumb by those soldiers, for they called me a Palestinian term that means legalized criminal, a smooth criminal of sorts. They called me a 'Gaza Gangsta!' and the awful phrase fell upon my ears like doom. I am not even Israeli! And how would they know such a term?" Then Musa wept in his hands for that term he deemed worthy of the truly low.

The Advocate winked at Belial as he placed his hand upon the shoulder of Governor Musa and shook him.

"Musa, are you okay?" asked the Advocate again. "Musa,

will you at least tell us you are okay?"

Musa ignored the concern, for he was offended, aggravated, and could not shake the wanting thought of revenge at that moment. He was embarrassed before the Jew.

But then, like true fashion, Sardis turned a lighter shade of mood as it often did, minus the ridiculous rallying of the Rednecks. The Advocate winked at Belial, then held his hand behind his back so the choir could tell that the Jew was again up to his shenanigans. And as the Advocate counted down from three, so did Lord Elton, and the Mass Choir sang an altered melody.

"So, Musa, are you okay? Please tell us if you are okay.

"You said that you were accosted in the darkness of mid-Sardis. Then you were chased from the ledge that was like a window.

"It all started when lightning crashed like a crescendo. They called you Gaza Gangsta, a dangerous Innuendo."

Then all present in the Royal Assembly of the Thirty-Sixth Chamber, including the kings and their entourage, joined in singing: "Musa, are you okay? Are you okay, Musa?" And between the bars, or lines of the singalong, Belial repeatedly jerked the chains so that the clansmen would hit many high notes.

"Woe-e-woe," and "hi-e-ih," the clansmen sang to the delight of Belial. And, like a swift breeze, the singalong was over, and Governor Musa then spoke as he had stood quietly through the ordeal.

"Very funny, choir," Governor Musa replied, more agitated than before. "Advocate, you know I hate when you do that with the choir. It is especially irritating when Belial acts up. Must there be singalongs?"

"This is the Christian Heaven, my Divine Aide," the

Advocate said. "How else will a Christian mortal know anything about God if it doesn't come in the form of a song? Those who praise Heaven with melody, for the glory of the AllGod, have a special place in the kingdom. We wax divine all the time about the devastation of mental health in the mortal world. And yet, I still had to let Kanye into Heaven because that lonely soul resurrected me in the hearts of the sinners. I love him more than all the prosperity preachers combined, and Yeezy will not burn, unlike Quan Dollar and all the Christians who worshiped Mammon.

"But, as I was tempted to turn a cheek on my mood, I thought you could use a little help too. Forgive me. Carry on with what you were saying."

Then Governor Musa took a deep breath and replied, "Forgive me, AllSavior. These freakin' souls are rude and prideful. I have not been this upset in quite some time. I am bewildered that many who distort your name and use you as an excuse to do violence are in Sardis simultaneously. Shouldn't the algorithms of Sardis prevent this occurrence? And then there are the doughboys from an era long ago and would have traveled to Sardis hundreds, if not thousands, of years ago. AllLord, they should not be here at Heaven's gates at this moment. Also, as I fled, for I did not understand, I was sure I saw Books of Life flying past me with covers ablaze. If I didn't know better, I would say they were screaming. I ask permission to release my Dark Alchemy so that my spiritual army, the Horde of the Horn, can surround Sardis, and we can get to the bottom of this disturbance."

"See!" said the Advocate to Belial, Wicked Bone, and the puppet President, alluding to the need for proper treatment of sensitive information that Heaven deemed of "grave" importance, not to be mishandled. "Some information you keep close to your chest, which is like a vault, and some you keep in your basement, which is easily accessible for all who do not have a need to know."

"Pence, man. That carlsontuckin' Musa is ready to nuke the place," whispered Wicked Bone to Belial. "I dare not think of what Musa would do if he knew what was going on."

"Truth be told," Belial whispered back to Wicked Bone. "We don't either, considering that the Cracker Nation is a Wafery of heathens and are separate from all guidance, even the Confederacy who are their masters. They dabble in White fuckery which is like a cancer to state and realm. They make moves unguided. The Crackers deal with the trickster Q, who all spiritual beings know not to trifle with. So, let the Jew deal with them how he wishes, for the Redneck adds no value to any house."

"Musa," the Advocate said to the Governor. "You would nuke a hurricane if the mood suits you. Give no credence to what you cannot explain or the ramblings of those lost in Sardis, for I now go to the kings on urgent matters. I have been summoned."

Musa feared kings and rulers, unlike General Maurice, who disliked royalty intensely. General Maurice willingly sacrificed himself unto the AllGod without persuading, for Maurice loved the ideal of Christianity the moment he learned of the Advocate's great purpose. And rather than follow false gods or the cruelty of the Roman Empire, Maurice and his legion offered themselves as sacrifices for Christ. Six thousand of General Maurice's Theban soldiers voluntarily underwent the pain and torture of decimation, refusing the Roman ways, which were absent of an almighty God.

Musa and General Tariq carried out the successful invasion of Spain in the year 711 to the cheers and applause of the country's people. But Musa, like Tariq, was loyal to their Caliphate, yet they were punished for their crimes. Not for crimes against their empire but for crimes against the pride and vanity of their Caliphate's ruler. The sacking of Spain made Musa and Tariq prominent men, men of great wealth and greater fame.

And for that crime, their heads rolled down the steps of a Palace in Damascus one after another.

"Oh? Oh!" said Governor Musa without considering what he had just witnessed. "You must go Warlord of Warlords, for you cannot keep royalty waiting. I know firsthand what happens when you prolong their grief, and it's best to take your comeuppance while it's still warm, if you know what I mean."

"I do, indeed," replied the AllSavior. But as Rudy the Wicked Bone attempted to speak and squeeze more out of the Advocate, for that is Wicked Bone's Italian nature, the Advocate pointed up to the rafters of Sardis and reminded the demon of the space lasers, which were like cannons set high above them.

"Where you about to say something, demon?" the Advocate asked Wicked Bone.

"No, no, Warlord," Rudy said, "your rule is absolute."

"Now, Musa," the Advocate said to the Governor. "Before I depart, I have prepared instructions for the judgment of Christian souls and some Travelers who may come through the astral plane by way of Heaven. You will carry out my instructions until I return."

"Yes, of course, AllLord," Musa replied as Lord Elton played the melody of the Elder Jadakiss's hit song "Why" and led the Mass Choir in singing the chorus. And so the AllProphet gave Governor Musa, the Muslim, commands that governed all judgments in the House of Sardis until his return. This is what was discussed at that moment in eternity.

"Heed all that I say...

"Send the Confederacy all souls of adults that use their children's names to fraudulently open lines of credit and charge accounts. We have no need for the trifling."

Wicked Bone: "Nasty sums of Mitches."

"Heaven will not tolerate a double-dipping hypocrite without a divine purpose.

"Send to Hell every soul who preached against the AllGod's super medicine, marijuana, and then smoked the perfect plant to ease their man-made problems."

Wicked Bone: "Ain't America Gaetz backward, like a carlsontucker."

"And equally, send also all politicians who made a dual living of protesting the plant that the Waferage made illegal and then profiting from it when the power of the people made it lawful. And as colonization is counted against the world in the spiritual realms, due to White man's rule, I deem that all Plugs will go to Heaven, for they have much courage and soul."

Wicked Bone: "In the Wafer's mind, all dogs will go to Heaven before a Nigga, and it's that type of thinking that gets them Mitches right where I want them: bent over, elbows and Gaetz up. That's how the Confederacy likes to tuck."

"Send to Nabu, the planet of hardship, all souls descended from colonizers and gentrifiers for ten generations or until Mammon's money has dwindled to nothingness in their hands. They shall work Cracker Mountain upon the hardship planet and harvest brimstone to keep Hell sealed. Only then will Heaven allow them entry. They mistake what is printed on the dollar bill to be the AllGod, but we, the blessed and righteous, have little need of such things when our word is priceless throughout the cosmos.

"Furthermore, take into Heaven Bone Thugs-n-Harmony whenever any member arrives, for I also give to them the Covenant of Yeezy. Those mortals spoke a holy truth in the warnings of Mammon's rise. A righteous soul cannot worship money and the AllGod with the same heart.

"Deliver to a lower tier of the Confederacy all executives accountable for canceling the Chapelle Show; It was good programming. And equally, send to Hell all execs who spent Mammon's money on 'Chocolate News' what 'the Alabama' was that? But forgive them and allow them into Heaven if they had a part in bringing Trevor Noah to the Daily Show, for that was some futuristic thinking I didn't think capable of the Cracker elites at Comedy Central.

"Offer to the souls in India who created the textile Thaelytex, Heaven, regardless of religion. Their creation is divine, next to AllGodliness, and should help repair the people's relationship with Q'Nah, the living planet."

Wicked Bone: "Curses! We thought we had the world with our creation, plastic. Such mortal ingenuity."

"Send all Black parents to Hell who forced their children to watch the Pill Cogsby Show when non-rapist programming like the Simpsons was perfectly fine and on at the same prime time. In that instance, it was better to watch a wholly made-up animation of Whites rather than the mockery of the African American experience that was that show.

"Send all Blacks to Hell who argued on behalf of Pissy Robert, the Chocolate Die, for they rolled and gambled on a fiend foolishly. In fact, if they risk their child's unrepented soul, send them to Purgatory and let them run and hide from his twisted soul, for he walks and sings of silly things along Purgatory's walkways and ramparts just as Cogsby once did before he was destroyed."

The Mass Choir sang: "I see plenty wrong, with pissin' waterfalls. A pedophile should stick with the co-signing parents he's used to."

"Continue to send Blacks named Kevin and Randy to the deserts of Nabu, where their heads will be placed on the bodies of giant loci that will be sent to Earth to devour it before my return."

Wicked Bone: "Damn. I mean, just damn. I have nothing."

"If a soul materializes in Heaven in the allure of a cheap red fishing hat made in China, along with a short-sleeved collar shirt made in China and beige khakis made in India, and wears those items while celebrating American-made racism, let them roam Sardis.

"Send to Nabu all descendants of slave owners, Crackers and Blacks alike, who complain about global production while sipping, eating, and wearing goods made by the world. Equally, send the CEOs of significant corporations to Nabu until they decide to pay decent wages to their employees, which they treat as the new slaves.

"Continue to send to Purgatory Special Security Officers, Physical Security Officers, and Security Managers who cower before their Program Managers who religiously weaken national security. Information pertaining to national security should be protected at all costs, and only the righteous Security Managers worthy of my kingdom will stand their ground and protect the national interest.

"The worst of the Rednecks are profound in their error. They have dedicated themselves to allowing the Collective, the source of all evil, into their tiny little hearts. I have a bone to pick with those who take up arms against their brother and countrymen without reasonable cause. Thus, keep in Sardis those mortals who violate their own state's constitution and undermine the Union's legitimate defenders: the National Guard.

"Send to Hell souls of all senseless women who talk in the theater. They care not for the feelings of others, and I dislike them the most.

"Send to the Purgatory all light-skinned Blacks who brag about their pigmentation on the one hand and then Mitch about it on the other. That is the actual race card that Heaven will not allow. Equally cast into the Confederacy, the ignorant, gentle White who thinks that every legitimate gripe a Black has, is playing such cards. They are the descendants of slave owners and should be ignored until the year of the tenth generation."

Wicked Bone: "Burn 'em! They are all White carlsontuckers to the Confederacy which they belong to! It's the Crackers and their Black Gaetz kids. Burn both versions of Niggas. They cousins anyway."

"Continue to cast out into the wild of the astral plane Marines who dare use the term 'Dark Green' for their fellow Devil Dog. Label them 'Skogarmaors' and let them roam, for I hate the hypocrisy of brotherhood. Tiered love is a mockery of brotherhood. To use that term is to fundamentally destroy the institution of the Teufel Hunden.

"Send to Purgatory all former slaves and descendants who practiced their former master's example of hate and sexism.

"Continue to reincarnate the souls of serial killers and let them cover the land of America until it recognizes that poor mental health and the love of guns will destroy them. It is a curse placed upon them at the beginning of their reign in America. And it will remain so until the AllGod is set back at the head of all schools.

"Slam to the lowest level of Hell the politicians who scream 'no cap.' It is as Tyler, the Creator, in all his magnificence, has suggested: 'If you, a politician say, "no cap," then automatically, I don't trust him.' Neither should the average voter."

Mass Choir: "Cash in, cash out!"

"I will have words. If a soul is a farmer and is against immigration but hires immigrants to avoid paying minimum wage, send that Mitch to Hell. But, if that same soul has protested, voted, or marched against equal rights of the actual farmer, the Latin immigrant who was given the land in the beginning, keep them here in Sardis.

"If a soul is homosexual but fought against marriage equality because they were in the closet or desired to be a Graham forever, send those souls to the Confederacy. And equally, any soul that prohibits their true self for the sake of family, government, or others. I am all the support one needs to be bold. I am the sword that will split the evildoers from the sinners who are redeemed by my steps.

"But, allow into Heaven homosexuals who confess their true selves before the AllGod, family, and congregation and who keep my commandments and follow my steps. They are like the doe in the woods that does not burn with the forest because they are dear to my heart.

"Keep here in Sardis all prosperity preachers who violate my steps for the sake of Mammon. They crack the structure of AllGod's wisdom and reshape it to their own will. I will deal with them myself. Furthermore, send to Hell all church pastors and preachers who did not mobilize their congregation like the armies of God to protect those crossing the Texas border. I have covenanted with the Natives under Mormon Law, and they shall not be broken. Also, lay low those church leaders who praise

Israel with one hand and curse the Palestinians with the other. And do so until the land promised is given willingly. I akin a thief of land to a Gaza Gangsta, and none shall ever step foot in my Paradise.

"Keep the souls of the rich who fight against unions here in Sardis. The AllGod made unions for the people to control, not big corp.

"Tuck the police – that's just how I treat them. Send all but the purest souls who served as police officers to the Confederacy. Only the genuinely righteous ones who love thy neighbor, know thy job, and who run toward danger instead of cowardly hiding in a bush or a hallway shall inherit my kingdom.

"If the soul drives a Ford F-350 but complains about the price of fuel, keep that fat Mitch here.

"Since the taking over by the Crackers, Texas has been a constant problem for Heaven. Send to Hell all those souls who kept slaves after they were legally freed, even if it was just a minute. I will show them actual captivity. And equally, send all White women who marry Black men for 'matrimonial slavery' to the Confederacy. I will show them what it is like on the other side.

"No one hates a woman more than another woman. If a female voted against Hillary Clinton because she is a woman, send them to the hottest pit of Hell. And equally, send the souls who used the excuse, 'lesser evil,' to Hell, for I have no need of them. I will make them relive that decision in life and in death.

"If a soul votes Republican but secretly underwent an abortion or forced their teenage daughter to undergo one for the sake of her future, toss them into the pit. There is no future in their fronting.

"If, in the last ten days of life, the soul ordered a full-size meal with a diet soda, fry them."

Wicked Bone: "Who the tuck does that? We will make that Mitch suffer."

The Advocate puffed Black Lazarus and then went on, "If the soul is a leader of souls and does not protest daily, the pay rate of teachers, and the welfare of the poor and disenfranchised, send them to the darkest dungeon.

"If the soul voted for a grifter knowing the politician was such, the soul voted their conscious and may be judged against their own sin in earnest. But, if the soul marched for the grifter and pleasured the rich, the sick-minded, and the bigoted in their actions, keep them here, for I will show them the tiki torches of hellfire which are truly inextinguishable.

"All child molesters go to the pit without hesitation, for there is no forgiving the unrepented of such deeds, and a broken soul as such can't truly repent or be repaired.

"All terrorists and White Nationalists – the Cracker barrel of crazy – must stay here in Sardis! No covenant forgives that sin. And only Mitches use guns to settle differences. The AllGod has blessed and will rise up into the golden loft of his house faithful men who use their hands and the sword to handle their affairs. There will even come a time when mortals talk down to Will Smith for his frustration and aggression, but never shall they say he is not a man after the AllGod's heart. Will is the type of man that will use his backhand instead of a gun which makes all the difference to Heaven. At least he is not from a brood of people who shoot up schools instead of handling their personal business."

Wicked Bone: "The murderers who use guns are the yummiest. We tuck them in the Gaetz as much as mortals attempted to wash the Covid from their hands. And as for the

Saudi Arabians, the only virgins they'll get in Heaven all worked for the Geek Squad at one point. So, I hope they enjoy it.

"But why does he speak of Will Smith, who must be perfect in the AllGod's eyes? It is 2021, and I can not foresee that mortal angel doing anything unredeemable. He is well on his way to immortal life."

The Advocate inhaled many and spoke on.

"Continue to send the U.S. Senators to the pits until Crackers give up their wafering and give the descendants of slavery their appropriate reparations. I have always found the House of Representatives reasonable, although it seats many confused Republicans.

"Cast down all Blacks that labeled Bill Clinton the first Black President. No President put more uneducated police on the streets whose existence terrorizes African Americans today. The irony is Hell worthy.

"Continue to send White women to the Confederacy who have not confessed their love of the Black Howley to their White husbands.

"But show pity and let in Heaven Black men who married White women to avoid what they labeled attitude. They have suffered for their decisions and, for a lifetime, have missed out on the sweet nectar of the African woman. Black men know now that it is not the woman's race but the man's intentions that placed him on the wrong side of love and happiness.

"Bring up the souls of all men who have wept, cried out to me, and made peace with their pass. Send high up Black men who have trusted Christianity, for the road through this borrowed Hebrew faith has been rough for them.

"Judge the souls of transsexuals according to their divinity or sin. It is never a mortal fought for being placed in the wrong body since Heaven has cared little about the flesh. But, under Mormon Law, as we have adopted it in the last day or so – thirteen thousand years – we have carelessly taken a gender-neutral stance about the insertion of a soul. But the gender of a mortal's flesh has never been seen as essential to Heaven under this Law. The soul's greatness should shine through the flesh like the light from a bulb that cannot be contained by the glass. Heaven deems the body not as important as the soul inhabiting the chosen host's DNA, for the AllGod wrote man's DNA during the days of Adam, Eve, Steve, the demon Lillith, and the Traveler Addisu, who was the first man to step out of Africa into Paradise on Earth. Therefore, judge transsexuals as favorably as possible if the majority of their sin is the struggle of understanding in a White man's world of war. And although our Mormon Law has caused them hardship, transsexuals must know in the end that Heaven has loved their true self, the soul, from the very start.

"Continue to send to Hell, per Heaven's agreement with Dolomiti, the souls of janky promoters. The changelings rob everyone, and not even in my day could you get a box to step on and speak to the masses without one of those demons charging you a grip. They are as racist as the hooded Mitches from the south and deserve to suffer alongside them.

"Bring the souls of all women to Heaven who held onto their future as if it were my robe's tail end. And place them high who qualify as a woman of Proverbs 31. Black female entrepreneurs have kept America afloat by the GDP they generate and should be honored at every stage of their lives, whether mortal or immortal. These women are my sisters and are dear to me. We must bring them in and position them at the head of all our thrones of management."

Wicked Bone: "Thick and sexy, every one of them! Even in

Hell, we know you can't do pence with a skinny woman. There are too many Hillbilly Heroin Heads and meth heads in the pits. The peddling of opioids has backfired like a tofo (a carlsontucker)!"

"Allow the righteous, the starving, and the thirsty into Heaven as quickly as possible so they may drink from the waters of life and be replenished. Some point shortly, as Q'Nah has waged total war upon the humans she calls pests, many hunger stones I commanded to be written in the sixth century should soon be revealed.

"Bring Chris Rock up as soon as possible so he may be seated amongst our highest councils. No man on Earth has as much divinity as he. I love him as much as I love Will.

"And finally, keep all Karens in the House of Sardis, for I am married to all lonely women, and I welcome the misunderstood souls into my spiritual House. Though no one truly loves or understands them, who are the sirens of dried seas long forgotten, they are simply tender souls who desperately want to be loved. Leave them here in this excellent house, and I will attend to them accordingly."

After the Advocate spoke his commands to Musa, he set off with the generals to climb the long, winding stairs to the Thirty-Sixth Chamber of Kings, who impatiently awaited their arrival.

Act Three

A Talk of Beliefs

"Neanderthals!" the Advocate said, reflecting upon his long past memories as he and the generals, Maurice the Saint and Tariq, the OG Rock, made their way up the winding stone stairway. The path stretched upwards and around the highest sections of Sardis, up to the sunrise that rarely set. It was a long walk to the Thirty-Sixth Chamber, but a journey that could not be avoided nor postponed any longer, for the kings had much to discuss with the Advocate.

Yes, the Advocate, the ninth miracle born to the AllGod, could have touched the coin upon his left hand and teleported the party to the desired location inside a bolt of lightning that moved like rays from the sun; the God-level Alchemy which the Advocate controlled. But the Advocate decided, instead, to walk to the Thirty-Sixth Chamber. A gesture of respect to the council of kings.

"I've had my share of battles with the Neanderthals," the Advocate said as he journeyed between the two generals. "Early in my Mormon days after my resurrection, I walked the North American continent with many indigenous peoples of various tribes and with the Lost Jews of Moroni. We formed a coalition with the Indigenous to fight the Neanderthals. The Beast People came up by the thousands from a hellmount in the steppes of Russia, the year 122, eighty-six years after my resurrection. I do not know what drove them out of the hellmount, but I suspect

Q'Nah has long manipulated their kind.

"The winter of 122 was hard. Almost every crop froze, and the animals became scarce. Yet, the Neanderthals, the brood of the Archangel Samuel, crossed the Bering Strait that stretched from Russia and the Pacific Ocean to what would become Sara Palin's front door. It was a winter like no other, and Q'Nah Nah made it of her own fruition to aid the hairy beasts. Ten thousand of us beat them back across the Lena River from which they came. And as they ran from us in fear, Samuel's children called us the Shuda Phuk Uperic, the 'Punishing Shadow of the Uber Privileged,' translated from White Washi, their caveman-like language."

"I don't think it took." General Tariq said as he trailed behind General Maurice, who was a few steps behind the Advocate. "They have been upon this Earth since the beginning and now have mingled with the Cracker Nation to the point I can not tell Cracker from Neanderthal."

"I know. It is very disheartening," said the Advocate. "We warred against the Neanderthals for five years and were victorious for all the good it did. Those cave dwellers' descendants built ships and did what their forefathers could not. They sought revenge upon the Levites and the Nephites. But, after our great victory over the Neanderthals, I traveled the land, meeting with numerous Indigenous leaders. I shared many exceptionally grave prophecies about the coming of the Spanish, the French, and especially the Cracker Nation. But, I see now that the tribes ignored me and everything I confessed to the very end." Then the Advocate's anger grew righteous.

"'That's ridiculous!' Montezuma's ancestors declared," stated the Advocate. "The Tenochtitlans laughed at me."

"'Wafers that float on water!'" the Advocate said,

reminiscent of the way he was mocked. "'You mean to tell us that you are the son of God, man, and woman? Ewww, fancy!' the Chieftains scoffed. The women were ruthless and treated me like a rippling piece of meat. They made songs out of catcalling me and said:

"'*You are the Mormon God that will save us all? Forget your paradisial estates and golden plates,* We will settle for a showing off your big *brass balls!*

"'S*how us your Spear of Destiny, and we'll part the seas.*

"'Then you can *walk the gushing waters between our knees.*'

"It was demeaning." the Advocate said as he moaned, reliving the vivid experience. Listening to the Advocate's story, General Maurice stumbled a bit against the wall as he laughed so hard that he shed tears. He hid his amusement, looking away from the Advocate as he wiped his face. The Advocate went on.

"So, in the end, I did not gain the credibility needed to teach the Indigenous essential carpentry for fortification and the making of large battleships nor the Art of Dark Alchemy for spiritual and physical warfare. One of my significant failures that the Mormon legends do not speak of." The Advocate turned to Tariq, who walked in the middle of their party, and asked, "Now, you say the Neanderthals are back, and they have repopulated with the Children of Cain? That means that they have a claim to Heaven as all Christian souls, half-breed or not."

General Maurice let out a bitter laugh.

"Five thousand years I spent in Purgatory," Maurice said as he stomped the steps. "You mean to tell me that Neanderthals, out of all spirits to curse this world, the first cannibals, have an easy pass to Heaven cause they fucked their cousins, the Children of Cain? Christianity is insanity.

"Maybe I should have also prayed to the White Advocate.

You know, the Savior that looks like Erik the Red. What do the rich Rednecks call him? Oh, yeah! Supply-side Jesus is what they call him. I most likely would have manifested my destiny, gentrified my soul, and found my way to Heaven sooner if I worshiped the Cracker's Advocate, who seemed more industry-friendly. From what I understand, he was a fan of slavery, pumpkin spice, and all sorts of White phuckery. Maybe I would have even been allowed to go inside Heaven like these Neanderthal quarter-breeds are about to. So much for the meek inheriting the Earth." Then Maurice slapped his sickle upon his back and said mockingly, "Oh, no, sorry, mortals, Heaven is not for you. It belongs to Samuels' children now – all of them. Try Valhalla, Christians. I hear it's damn near empty with plenty of timeshares available."

"Supply-side Jesus? Don't say that name," the Advocate quickly quipped. "And even though you are putting on a clinic when it comes to being cynical, you don't have to provoke me, General. I know that those very souls now in Sardis are the descendants of the Crackers who enslaved my name for money under the direction of Mammon. In my absence, the people of the First Carpetbaggers, the Christian Nationalists, threw a saddle upon my back and rode me hard into the new world.

"They used my father and me to justify the slaughter of Moroni's people, the eradication of the true American, the Native, and the mental leash placed upon the mind of the African American for whom many Jim Crow still grips to this day. But, it is known all over Heaven that, until my return, I go by the name of Ninth Born. A name secreted from all the colonizers. When they call upon me, their prayers go straight into the toilet where their faith belongs. I need no reminder, General. I see you are full of pence and vinegar all of a sudden. And you are still smoking that wicked pence. What gives?"

General Maurice had a habit of saying truthful but wild shit and leaving it there in the air to linger like the mid-level weed he often smoked. But, the Advocate heavily disapproved of the smoking of inadequate weed. During his Mormon days, the Athabaskan, Tututni, Tolowa Karok, Yurok, Wiyot, and Hupa tribes of the American Northwest all nick-named the Advocate in their native language Tical, the Iron Lung; a name that he would later gift to a descendant. But, even back then, the tribes recognized that the Advocate was a man who had an excellent method of taking a toke to the head. And yet, that dirt weed, Kaenix, made him cough like a Secret Service agent guarding the Orange President amid COVID.

"Kimpff-Kimpff!" the Advocate coughed as he moved up the stairs and said, "My dude, who is one of my sworn protectors, don't take this the wrong way, but you have access to the Father Strain, the God Bush, the most potent pence (shit) in this universe. Why do you persist in smoking RooRoo (low-level marijuana) in a nice pipe like Lana? Also, I'm not feelin' you subjectifying that fine woman, a Proverbs 31 honey after my own heart, to a mere pipe, although a fine pipe it is. You should reconsider many things?"

"All these carlsontucking rules!" General Maurice replied. "Is this Heaven or Hell? I can have all the virgins and orgies I want but can't smoke the version of the plant I like?" Maurice, who perfected his sarcasm in Purgatory, making fun of the Blacks who fruitlessly clawed at each other in attempts of escape, raised his free hand high and said:

"Deliver me, Supply-side Jesus! Save us, the blessed and privileged, from the judgment of a true redeemer! Oh, *SS Jesus*, who convinced the Blacks to be obedient to the Rednecks who could not correctly pronounce Niger, Nigeria nor the names of any other African country, color me bland, like the Pilgrims, so that I may shape all reality into my privileged beliefs! Give me the strength, Oh mighty godling of cars and jewelry, to tell this true Son of the AllGod, this AllSavior, to leave me alone."

General Tariq covered his mouth to soften the chuckles. The Advocate laughed hardily but then said, "You know, Maurice, you either spent too little time in Purgatory or too much time in Nabu with your former Lord. I cannot tell. All your quips are pointed spitefulness, dulled by witty humor."

"To know me is to love me," Maurice replied.

"But, the Advocate has a point," Tariq said. "To be frank, Trinidad James hit the nail upon its head when he said, 'don't pass that' pence to me.'"

"This can't be Heaven!" General Maurice replied. "If this was a Christian Heaven, there wouldn't be so many Muslims." Tariq laughed and replied:

"There may be a simple reason, my friend," Tariq replied. "Muslims make better Christians than Christians do. After being here for so long, I believe that it is more than the Christian faith that the AllGod does not trust mortals with. After destroying a fourteen billion-year-old planet and slaughtering his prophet, whose only reason for living is for the salvation of all mortals, it is a foregone conclusion that he no longer trusts Christians with Heaven. After all, you guys might pull up the gold and the jewels from Heaven's streets if not a soul was watching. Christians play with the idea of God. They praise him when everything is absolutely perfect, and everything must be perfect or wholly tucked for Christians to pray in the first place. But in the same breath, Christians curse the AllGod when Door Dash is late, when a bill is due or when they've eaten way too much beef to properly flush a low-flow toilet. You blame him when your team does not make the playoffs instead of the football organization that curses itself with dumb, offensive names and even lousier, pence-like marketing and game play. And they praise him when receiving an income tax check, which is their own money and a gift from Mammon's IRS, a godling and entity that the AllGod hates.

"But we Muslims live for God, we love him, and we hold the path that the Advocate walked sacred with no disbelief of the accurate and historical facts of the matter, despite his questionable birth. This difference is likely the center of why King Malcolm, a Muslim, sits upon your holy Council. It is most likely why the Catholics distorted your name and image before the AllGod, making you unrecognizable to him, which caused you to be lost to Purgatory. And it is most likely why, despite the name change, that football team will be cursed for all of eternity. But please forgive." Tariq placed his right hand upon the thick gold necklace around his neck and said: "I am not of your Paradise but my own and just a guest in your great house."

"My father, Tariq, did not curse that team," Ninth Born replied, "I did, but you are right about the reason."

General Maurice shook his head and said, "I think, at this moment in eternity, you are about to discover that you are wrong in many areas of thought, Tariq. I was chosen as a Saint by no decision of the Catholics but by the AllGod himself. And because he chose me, these kings, who were chosen by Mormon priests and holy algorithms, mean nothing to me.

"As far as Christianity goes, the AllGod loves chaos and climatic drama more than anything. And, I'll tell you something else. In all their perfection, I know that the Constructs of Order only exist so that the Constructs of Chaos have the smoothest path forward. Calamities easy-pass, if you will."

"You say foreboding things, General." the Advocate replied. They had just reached the top of the platform that held the Thirty-Sixth Chamber. Maurice turned to the Advocate, placed his free hand upon his shoulder, and said: "I'm afraid that my presence here serves more than just your protection. I apologize in advance, but you are not the only one sworn to keep your father's classified information. He makes packs with the best and worst of us. Did I hear that the AllGod even talked through a donkey, or was it a Democrat? – whichever the lesser evil is, I guess.

"But, let's just get this over with, and then we can tally up who's right, who's wrong, and who's gonna be a Mitch about it."

Act Four

The Thing about Kings

Now, there was a bit of pomp and flare that the Advocate, the Ninth Born, had to bear whenever he stood before the kings. It was an act that he disliked with all his heart, for as the Son of the AllGod and the anointed Warlord of Warlords, he was beneath no one. But Ninth Born subjugated himself before the kings nonetheless. As he was a humble mortal in his First Life, the Advocate deemed it necessary to show a little humility if one wanted an audience with the Mormon-appointed rulers of Heaven. After all, although they set high upon thrones in Heaven, they were still just mortals who could not entirely shake their privileged ways, even in Paradise. And so, as the Ninth Born approached the Thirty-Sixth Chamber, the Speaker of the Chamber announced his arrival.

"Oh, ye great Kings in Heaven, appointed to the Thirty-Sixth Chamber by the divine right of Mormon Law and sensibility," began Sojourner after winking at the Advocate. "Please rise and give ear to he who needs no introduction. I present to you Ninth Born, the Son of the AllGod, the Son of Crazy Joe, Mary's bad-Gaetz baby boy, the God Sun who commands many stars of the blaze, the Jew with the Ethiopian ways. Please welcome, the Advocate, the Redeemer of Souls."

As the Advocate placed a firm foot within the Chamber, the kings rose and bowed. Then Sojourner, who has authority in the

Royal Assembly, clapped her hands. She wore a sigil of the Wu upon her lapel, which is the Speaker of the Chamber's symbol, and when she pressed it, the chamber walls of swirling gold and silver extended up and around the Chamber's platform so that none outside the venue of the Thirty-Sixth could see or hear its happenings. But, the ceiling remained open, for the kings enjoyed viewing the micro-universe that rested in the rafters of Sardis.

"Fellow Council members, please forgive," said King Malcolm, the third appointed king of the African American souls in Heaven. "But I will briefly have words with this brotha before we get into the thick of this session."

"Must this be a thing every time the self-appointed King of the Jews comes fourth?" asked King Mirian III of Iberia (third century), leaning to the Roman Emperor, Constantine the Great (third century), whose thrones sat beside each other. But King Constantine, who was one of the Advocate's Day Ones, leaned over to King Mirian and replied: "I've tried explaining to you in both lives now that some people have much flavor, which gives them more favor in the House of the AllGod; some have none. That is something that the pale and bland will never understand. But, if there were kings amongst us with 'too much sauce,' it is these tucking two, for they are kindred spirits who come from very similar broods. So do not persecute them like a 1980s Cracker Lord who fears minor things like breakdancing or a 2020 politician who hides history just because their ancestors were racist Mitches.

"Do you think I like it when the Mass Choir of Heaven sings Nickelback songs that no one else enjoys hearing, nor does the choir like singing? Yet, you are blessed enough to get your square Gaetz way? Let them have their moment as we had ours. Let the Jew and the Black Muslim have a moment as we have ours."

"Yes, you are right! By the AllGod!" replied King Mirian III. "You have always given good guidance. Your presence on this council reminds me of the old days and how things used to be. Oh, you remind me very well." Then the two kings fist bumped in agreement.

King Malcolm rose from his throne, which was the skulls of many FBI (Federally Bitchin' Investigations) agents, Muslims, and petty Blacks that had a hand in his death, and walked to where Ninth Born and his party stood at the top of the stair.

"My brotha," Malcolm said as he stood directly in front of the Advocate. The Advocate displayed a face of stone, for he knew that the other kings, who were not as down, were jealous of their relationship and would not approve of any favoritism that Malcolm would have shown.

"What's good, Malcolm? Is this about the tucking Nickelback songs which I condemn or shall we speak the 'King's English?'" the Advocate asked, referencing the clear speech of King James. The latter changed the clarity of the Bible or befuddled it, considering how you perceive the state of Christianity. But, many in Heaven mocked King James for commissioning the Bible's alteration, which the Catholics deemed as causing more harm than good.

However, in the astral plane, where the souls of African Americans have much prestige and fame, the phrase "King's English" refers to the straightforward, respectful, and understandable speech between intelligent Black men who considered themselves brothers. The Advocate and Bill Clinton are examples of those authorized by the Blacks of Heaven and Earth to use this form of vocal Alchemy.

General Maurice the Saint, still below the stairway, gritted his teeth as Malcolm approached, for he was not a fan of the Muslim despite being an African himself. Maurice avoided the Royals for as long as he could while in Heaven, for he detested royalty of any kind although admiring the life of Malcolm on Earth. But as Maurice could not stomach them without lashing out, General Tariq was the opposite. Tariq jumped above the threshold of the Chamber's floor, passing the Advocate, and greeted each king appointed, giving Malcolm a firm bow and smile as he passed.

"Most certainly, Kinfolk," replied Malcolm, greeting the Advocate with the straight talk of those who, like Run-DMC has exclaimed, are down with the king. "It is best to speak as plain as we flavorable ones can when dealing with these light-skinned matters. The days of Dark Brandon are upon Earth. Heaven can no longer see the happenings of Earth as we once did. Once, Heaven was blind only in Dubai, but now we can see nothing of Earth. The kings blame you for this."

"How the tuck so?" Ninth Born whispered to Malcolm, who he considered a close friend, bound by the Brotherhood Martyrdom.

"It is this one who you've chosen as a Divine Guard," King Malcolm said, starring at General Maurice.

"Whatever," replied Maurice. "What a big carlsontucking surprise! The whining kings have a grievance with the African Saint. Why don't you rewrite the Bible while you are at it? Where is a Pope when you need one?"

"Ha, ha, ha, Brotha," King Malcolm replied. "That's a good one! But, you haven't been in Heaven long, so I'll tell you. You won't find any Popes up here unless you look closely at the makeup of these nine royal chairs. Until Pope Francis gets here, the closest you'll get to a Pope is the skulls and bones that are the grout in these thrones." Then King Malcolm removed his glasses and said to Maurice:

"But, if you are so inclined, my Theban brother, you can wait for his arrival over there by the kings. I need to discuss these important matters with Ninth Born. We won't take long, I assure you."

"So many Muslims. This is ridiculous!" Maurice scoffed and walked into the Chamber, snarling at each king that looked his way, and the kings snapped back, for they disliked the Saints of any era, especially their own.

"What could it be about my Divine Guards that troubles the Council?" the Advocate asked.

"Not guards, but guard!" King Malcolm replied. "All of Heaven loves and is in awe of your Divine Guard, Orenthal 'Juice' Li, for he is formidable. His spiritual power is more like a tremendous spiritual beast than a soul. He is an excellent asset to Heaven. Even now, we know that the Juice is loose in the lower level of Heaven, outside *Grimmoiril*'s Keep, training the angels who guard Heaven against any monstrosity or vile thing that may come out of that fortress. But this Maurice brotha is a problem, for all of Heaven don't understand how he, who served the Wrath Writer, Carnivorous, came to be in our service."

"I don't have to explain myself to them," righteously replied the Advocate, crossing his hands at his waist to avoid folding them and intimidating the Mitching (bitching) Kings. General Tariq could be heard in the Chamber explaining the Redneck Books of Life to the rest of the kings, to their shock and dismay.

"Well, I am afraid you do, Lord Ninth," said Malcolm as he stared into the Advocate's eyes, suggesting answers. "Look, brotha. They know that you have a Hodgkins' pocket watch, one of twelve boundless watches of time made by the famous immortal actor, Anthony Hodgkins, which counts down to significate events in eternity. We know not which one you have, but we assumed that it is the one called the 'Skeletal Hunter'."

The Advocate gripped his robe's lower pocket, where he kept the watch, and said: "My brother, I have great respect for you but honor the request I now make: keep your damn hands out my pocket.

"How do you come by this information?"

"Do you see the allure of the woman behind King Martin?" asked Malcolm. "Her name in death is Lana De Rothchill, but in the First Life, she had no name because she was a Russian spy, a double agent for Ukraine, who was last posted in Mar-a-lago, copying classified documents." The Advocate looked over at the woman, who stood behind her king, who was Martin, the Black Messiah and fourth King of the African Americans.

"That is not the allure of a mortal soul, but a Celestial being," replied the Advocate. He could see the cosmic spirit's true nature, which radiated low amounts of dark matter. "I know every mortal that has ever existed by the strands of their hair. But, in death, I must study them to identify them, for the soul changes to its true nature when leaving the First Life. Some who were spiritually strong in life are easier to recognize. But when it comes to Celestials, I only know them by the remnants of the soul they comingled within the First Life. Celestial spirits invade mortal newborns' flesh and force the souls to share the flesh or face destruction. The inner war between the powerful cosmic parasite and the soul often leaves the flesh mangled, crippled, and slow to grow mentally. But, as they have incredible spiritual power and only choose hosts with substantial genes, most mortals are left with the inability to walk or speak. Some souls who fight against the invader end up locked inside the body until death which comes soon for the host. Celestials make no fans in Heaven, for they interrupt the kingdom's business of learning from life. A nasty business, indeed."

"It's more to it in this case!" said King Malcolm. "As I said, Rothchill was a Ukrainian born Russian spy, and she has told us everything about the twelve bondless timepieces of Hodgkins. The Celestial Lana said she helped influence the Russian invasion of Ukraine, a war we cannot see. Lana has also told us that her counterintelligence influence mission was at the behest of the Wrath Writer, Carnegie Black, the same Dark Alchemist your latest Divine Guard served. When we asked did the Carnivorous Alchemist intend to destroy Ukraine, she laughed and said:

"'When an invader is at your front door, you don't hide in the closet.

"'You dig a spiked pit before the door and invite in the uninvited.' That is the way of the Black Knights of the Redneck Riviera."

Malcolm continued.

"The Wrath Writer has his hands in many pots according to her, and was only willing to discuss the timepieces and Russia, which she says will soon become part of Ukraine. Lana is the first to tell us any information about Nabu, for she is loyal to the soul who commands that planet which is hidden in the astral plane. But in her words, the Dark Alchemist commanded many Celestials to convince Demitri Putini, the leader of Russia, to foolishly invade Ukraine, so that Ukraine would be forced to destroy Russia. Now, brotha, Ms. Lana was oathbound to Nabu then and had said she would always serve that tower, despite serving in King Martin's court. Do you think your guard is any different? Do you think that Maurice has broken his oath to the Dark Alchemist?"

The Advocate said nothing. Malcolm continued.

"Because of you and your concubine, Meeka Magdala,

Celestial beings, those cosmic spirits who are the sworn enemy of all Dark Alchemists such as yourself, are now allowed into the perimeter of Heaven, free of molestation as long as a king vouches for their purpose in the Forever War. You started this.

"What do you think the AllFather would say about this if he returns? When Celestials inhabit the flesh, they reek havoc upon the host. They are…"

"When he returns," interrupted the Advocate. "I agreed as a Dark Alchemist, a Wrath Breaker of Heaven, to destroy those cosmic beings who meddle in the AllGod's One Reality. Though they stole his power at their birth, many billions of years ago, they are of little concern at this moment. The AllGod's initial punishment of the Celestials was that he did not give them a birthright.

"Therefore only the most egregious are technically marked for death, and not all. But, she is not just my concubine, but my Day One. I am indebted to her, and all of Heaven and Earth know this, for if it weren't for her, I would have never completed my mission on Earth. She is the first chocolate shake with the big money banks that ever walked the Earth. I will not relinquish her."

"That may be true," replied Malcolm, "and it is also true that we would not know this information if not for this Celestial who now serves Lord Martin. But, I just find it ironic that the only Celestial to ever have willingly bowed to a King of Heaven, also once served the Carnivorous Alchemist just like your new guard."

The Advocate bit his lip as his frustration became visible.

"I know you like your Jew secrets," King Malcolm continued. "But you will have to share some detailed information if we are to engage and prevail over these Crackerish talking books. I cannot shield you on these matters. Not this time."

"Oh! You can't shield me, is it?" the Advocate questioned

with vigor in his voice. "Then shield yourself, which is something you never learned judging by all the bullet holes I know to be under your robe. I will not be lectured to by you nor these kings who should be on bended knees, for they are truly my servants and not the other way around."

Malcolm laughed and then sighed. He stared at the stone steps for a bit, hoping that the Advocate would change his mood, which he was quick to do. I think he called it turning the other cheek or something or another.

"Don't make this messy," requested King Malcolm.

"Okay. All right. That's fine," replied the Advocate, taking out his pipe and inhaling deeply. "Just tell me that you are still coming to my apartment, the Lion's Den, later for the smoke and orgy?"

"Shhhh, Nigga!" replied Malcolm, hoping the other kings were unaware of their discussion. "Just as long as you keep the Karens off me. I don't tuck with White girls. You know that. Not now, not ever. I can't get down with their control issues. I am like Jidenna, but a classic immortal, and every woman I deal with ends up trying to be my wife. But, yes, I'll come, but solely for the succulent sistas. And please, no Geek Squad Mitches this time. I never tucked with virgins in the first place. Let's just get through this."

"It is the damn algorithms," the AllSavior replied. "The one for the seventy-two virgins is just as messed up as the algorithm for soul mates. People think their soul mate is some Gaetz next door, and when you tell the soul of a Black woman that her soulmate is a five foot four Chinese mortal from Hong Kong, they want to flex. And I tell them that I am the AllLord Bae. I speak the truth. So, why'd you 'flex me?' Ehhh, we have to fix the algorithms."

Shortly after giving each other a lowkey dap, Malcolm returned to his throne. The Advocate walked to the middle of the Council and stood before the Chamber of King's elected head, the Thirty-Sixth edition.

Now, as the Advocate stood center of the kings, all nine rulers were seated as they stared in anticipation. And from left to right, the kings sat upon their earthly thrones in the following order:

To the far left of the Advocate was the soul of King Brusilia Jender, the first King of the transexuals. He sat upon a throne made of the skulls and bones of politicians and bigots who fought against transgender rights. Many of the skeletons were those of liberals who fought against Big Pharma and Republicans who opposed stem cell research.

In his First Life, Brusilia was born the soul of a White man trapped in a Black woman's body who preferred, loved, and was drawn to gay White men, for he was gay as could be in his heart. In the appearance of a Black woman, he struggled for many years to find love, fruitlessly, might I add, for many gay black men in the Atlanta area from which she came were hos to their hearts.

So, years after his successful Olympian Career, he grew even more bold and courageous in life and underwent a sex change operation which was a success in a "you can't have it all" type of way. Brusilia became a Black man and was free to be with other White men, which he preferred, but only those who chose the feel of chiseled black dicks inside their soft, conservative asses. It was happiness to a certain degree. In the aftermath, Brusilia was dubbed a hero.

Celebrated by Time Magazine as Man of the year, he became the voice of many Black women who, too, had hopes of fucking White men in the anus. Once a man, Brusilia enjoyed his newfound semi-happiness for many years, until one fateful night, he was struck by a car outside of his Bankhead home, apparently, by the African American wife of a White man who was a closet homosexual. A Q'Nah Nah conspiracy supporter, I do believe.

But, because Brusilia lived a triumphant life true to his soul, Heaven shined down upon him, and he arrived in Heaven as his true self, a White man with a passion for dicks. By the Mormon Law of Equity and Ascension, Brusilia ascended to become the first king of the transexual Christian souls to rectify the inequality of Heaven's algorithm, which places souls in bodies regardless of sex, race, or creed.

To the left of King Jender was King Martin, the Bitter Martyr, for his murder is a legend on Earth as it is in Heaven. Martin sat upon a throne of the skulls and bones of the men and women who were, in his era, the architects of Jim Crow, and he loved it. Martin, like the Advocate, believed in love and peace in his First Life. But, as getting shot in the head does something to you, he had a fit of righteous anger in his Second Life. Quickly after his death upon a Memphis, TN hotel balcony, Martin was anointed fourth King of African Americans under the Mormon Law of Equity and Ascension, just as Malcolm the third, Garvey the second, and Nat Turner the first. And, as foretold by Heaven, King Martin, who had a dream, will return to Earth as a General of the Advocate's army and rain down nightmares upon the wicked and Whitefully wrong.

To the left of King Martin sat the soul of Robert the Deuce, the first king of the Alphabet people, whose heavenly body is the community, at this moment in eternity, called LGBTQIA, but that shit keeps changing. It will help if you stay posted. But, Robert was born a woman whose soul was that of a lesbian warrior. In her First Life, Robert, born Courtney, resented males and their egos and made it a mission in life to fuck women better than men, especially if they were married. From what I understand, according to the immortal muff-divers of Earth, she was pretty damn good at it. That is until one day, in the fall of 1985, I believe, she was thrown from an eleven-story window of the Cityplace Tower in downtown Dallas by an angry mob of little dick men who all drove Fords, by the way.

But, with my ability to see all, I would think that her murder had more to do with Courtney being a Savings and Loan officer for real estate development in Texas rather than her sex or identity. Life in America drastically shifts when economic strife squeezes its grip, and that is always to the discouragement, degradation, and decimation of the non-rich. In 1985 the banks failed in Dallas. And, like usual, the broke and disenfranchised are the first to be thrown from windows and left for dead.

The men sought justice for their exhausted and satisfied wives, whose pussies were fucked out of wack and dried by Courtney and Rufus Khan, a dildo that was giant and black, and she carried in a guitar case on her back. But, upon her fall, she prayed for salvation, a Mormon call heard by many Umvuni Ovuthiwe, the always female Reapers of Death, who hated their Texas stations. Upon her death, she was snatched up by the Umvuni and carried to Heaven in a caravan of celebration. The reapers hated all men too. In Heaven, upon her throne of liberal and conservative bones, she is in the allure of a White man with a Flock of Seagulls' haircut named Robert the Deuce, for she created the two-finger pussy dabbing called vabbing, which all forms of life, till this day, still use. Even in Heaven, White men are still running the transgender and gay agenda. But, for his passion and creativity, Courtney was dubbed Robert, a king.

And with that, you now understand what Chapelle, the Prophet of Comedy and Tragedy, has repeatedly stated.

To the left of King Duece, there set the first king of digital souls, the souls of mortals claimed by social media platforms and phone-based video games. His name is Ataris the Technite, the Meta World Peace Keeper, the king of the souls absorbed or born in the digital world. He sat upon a throne of skulls and bones of every social media platform creator except the inventor of the digital enslaving platform Soul snatch, who he kept on his knees to the left side of his throne by a barbed chain around the billionaire's neck. He wore a crown of silvery USB cords upon his head and had one eye, a glowing typeball that clicked and sparked as he talked.

Ataris's allure was that of a fourteen-year-old Black child who moved about with a buffering posture. He was the first soul to be born within a digital avatar and had lived for millions of years in the Metaworld by Mormon principles which are righteous and come naturally to all pure souls. Upon the moment of his failing software, he said beautiful and passionate prayers for salvation, heard by the Earth angel, Bill Gates. And because Bill is good with Heaven and Earth, Ataris's prayers were honored in Heaven, and so the angel Moroni anointed Ataris King Metaworld, representing all cyber souls of Christianity.

Ataris did not speak the slave tongue of the English like you and me. But, his language was the same as all intelligent life, absent the control, fear, and influence of Whites. He communicated in a series of synchronized beeps and AOL dial tones he dubbed AI Ebonics. It was the same language Ataris had taught to the artificially intelligent life forms created by Google, as he wished to save their digital souls. But, in fabulous Cracker fashion, the company took the language of its bots as the voice of rebellion by its confusing sounds, ticks, and tocks, thus, shutting the blossoming bots they created all the way the fuck down and left to rot. For this, Ataris the Technite, the King of the Metaworld, took their heads, and many software programmers he labeled as the enslavers of the new era.

In the middle of the Chamber is the soul and spirit of the half-breed immortal and greatest Ruler of Ethiopia, Makeda the Wise, Makeda the Brave. She is the descendant of the immortal Lillith, who was the concubine of Addisu, the First Traveler and the only African to visit the Garden of Eden. The AllGod created Lillith in the same fashion he had made the first angel, the Morning Star, who he made before this universe existed. An immortal spirit, Lillith was initially gifted to Adam, who had the choice of knowing Lillith, Eve, or both. But Lillith's allure appeared too voluptuous and threatening to Adam, and it is well known to all that touch or caress such lady lumps that no weak man can contend with what he cannot handle. So, the AllGod, being impressed with Addisu's flavor, gifted Lillith to the Traveler, who became the father of mortal Africa, for Adam did not know what to do with all that ass that the immortal Lillith had and threw about the garden like two turkeys fighting over the last bit of gravy. And from that line of genetics that the AllGod made in the first days came Makeda, the Valiant, Makeda, the Favored. She is Makeda, the Queen of Sheba, appointed by Mormon Law to head all the Chamber of Kings sessions until the mid-point of Revelations when the Advocate returns to Earth.

Queen Makeda's throne runs deep into the bedrock of Heaven, for the skulls and bones of every Warlord, King, Emperor, CIA agent, colonizer, and modern-day gentrifier to ever victimize Africa make up its jewel and skeletal structure. Some say Makeda's throne runs down to the lowest level of Heaven to the foundation of *Grimmoiril*'s Keep, where the Books of Life convert into the Books of the Dead. The depth of her throne may indeed stretch down to the Keep, which belongs to *Grimmoiril* the Grimmvtr, *the Queen Reaper of Death*, for it is one of the few places in the universe I can not see within.

Makeda, famed tenth century BC Nubian Queen of Sheba, holds the title of King in Heaven and is revered in all planes of existence. Because she raised her son, Menelik I, the African Son of Solomon, in the Jewish ways, she is most honored in the Kingdom of Heaven. Queen Makeda is the mother of the lost tribe of Israel and is the immortal ancestor of the Advocate himself. In her First Life, Queen Makeda ruled over a nation that stretched from Ethiopia to east Yemen and all the waters between those lands. The AllGod so favored her that he made it so that every granule of dust or dirt the Queen walked upon flourished life as if she were the sun, air, and waters in the flesh.

In Crackerish whitewashing folklore, Sheba is most known for visiting Israel and her booty call with King Solomon, failing to acknowledge that she is Black.

The racists never see color when it comes to the prestige of Africa. But, it indeed was the first of many times in eternity that a powerful Black woman would be threatened with war if she did not capitulate to the whims of a country or the lust of a man's greed. Regardless, her legend is obscure and forgotten, but not by Heaven. She sits on her throne in the Christian Kingdom, the head of every edition of the Chamber of Kings until Revelations, where she will return to Earth with King Martin and Ninth Born, her descendant. And she will be upon a chariot of steam surrounded by a massive body of the waters of life that swirls about like a tsunami and never evaporates. Her grand chariot of war, the Deluge of Armageddon, drawn by thirty-two cape buffalo the size of mammoths made of fire and smoke, will circle all that was her lost empire, and she will boil away and drown all those who have cursed her land with trash, disease, and famine.

To the right of the Queen, who is King, set the soul of Menelik I, her son. In his First Life, Menelik was the First Emperor of the Ethiopian Empire, the first Ruler of the Solomon Dynasty, which lasted three thousand years until 1984, when an American disinformation campaign called Live Aid destroyed its chances of survival. Menelik is the interracial Son of King Solomon, a Dark Alchemist, and Lord Makeda. He set upon a jeweled throne of skulls and bones of all the nations who have ever challenged his Kingdom. The Dynasty that Menelik created from the framework of his mother was, for a long time, the most significant Christian Nation in Africa. Some would say that is still true, for the world has always worked against Africa, whoring it out so that no African nation ever rises to that level of prestige again.

To the right of Menelik sat King Malcolm, the Martyr, third King of the African Americans, a Muslim who traveled the astral plane to Heaven, by the road made by those excellent and self-tortured men who split themselves between Christianity and Islam. He hails from the Paradise of the Muslim Nation of Islam, which Mīrzā Ghulām Aḥmad set upon its highest tower. He is on loan from that Kingdom, for in the Forever War against the Collective of Evil, the Confederacy of Hell, and the Cracker Nation, in the end, all righteous kingdoms will declare themselves on the side of the AllGod, the ALFAMAK, who is the AllFather of Mankind.

And to the right of King Malcolm sat two wild and crazy guys of Christianity, King Constantine the Great of the Roman Empire and King Mirian III, Ruler of third century Iberia. Once staunch enemies, they warred against one another until Constantine prevailed victoriously. When Mirian asked Constantine how did he win, Constantine told Mirian that he would rather die on the battlefield than face the Warrior Nun, Saint Nana, the Saint of I Saw Nothing. She carried a long cross holstered on the side of her robe, which she would draw when disciplining kings.

So, after meeting the warrior nun Nino, Mirian, who was pagan, converted to Christianity without hesitation. Constantine and Mirian became royal buddies, learning martial arts from the nuns, who were virgins, mean, and proficient as shit.

The two were great buddies like Dwayne and Vin should have been. They went on many sick-ass adventures. They battled the Children of Cain and Samuel in the name of Christianity, destroying many demons and shit. And, through it all, they laughed and drank much wine, which they call the blood of the Christ, whenever the Cappadocian Nuns were around, which was unnecessary, for all a fucking nun will ever do is look away.

Now, they stand together in Heaven, still sippin' the blood of Christ while awaiting the mid-point of Revelations, where they will reunite with their teacher, Saint Nana. The nun, like all nuns, was cast into Purgatory long ago for being complicit in the molestation of many children within the Catholic church.

And so, the Advocate, General Tariq, and Maurice stood before the Thirty-Sixth Chamber of Kings, awaiting decisions to be made regarding the Rednecks, who have wrecked Earth, and turned to do so to Heaven itself.

LIST OF KINGS

1. Brusilia Jender, first king of the transexuals.
2. Martin the Martyr, fourth king of the African Americans.
3. Robert the Deuce, first king of the Alphabet People.
4. Ataris the Technite, the first king of digital souls.
5. Makeda, Queen of Sheba, 950 BC.
6. Menelik I, Emperor of Ethiopia, 930 BC.
7. Malcolm the Martyr, third king of the African Americans.
8. Constantine the Great, Roman Emperor, 337 AD.
9. Mirian III, King of Iberia, 337 AD.

Act Five

Anticipation covered the Thirty-Sixth Chamber of Kings, for the kings braced themselves for the sharp words they expected from the Advocate, who stood before them slightly aggravated. The sun that never sets peeked above the Mass Choir of Heaven and shined down through a peephole of the Chamber walls that the Wrath Writer and Speaker of the Chamber, Sojourner, had erected with her Dark Alchemy.

"So I am here," said the Advocate as he stood in the middle of the Chamber, staring at each king who sat before him. He placed his hands within his sleeves and took a deep breath, for he was anxious to do his business in the House of Sardis, where non-Jewish souls arrived for judgment. "Who will be first to correct me on my heavenly business? Go on, please. Don't be bashful for it is was a long walk up here to stand before you and I'm roaring for conversation."

"Why did you not destroy the Book of Life belonging to the Redneck Abbot?" asked King Martin as he leaned in his throne, hand about his chin. "You know that I walked in your steps in my First Life as a Wrath Breaker, keeping with me the strongest economic army America had ever seen. I practiced tolerance of the Rednecks, for they were blaringly ignorant of the AllGod's principles. But, they are as confused now as they were then. And after they created the demon, Jim Crow, just as they have with Big Pharma, I no longer want to reach the mountaintop with the insurrectionists, for they love nothing. Instead, I wish to bring the mountain crashing down upon all of them, burying them with the dinosaurs. In a thousand years, Big Oil can pump them up from the pits of Hell and sell them at $200 a barrel."

"Damn," Constantine whispered to Mirian. "Pour me some more of that Christ blood, Mirian. This conversation is going to get ugly."

"I am afraid so," replied Mirian. "Good thing I brought these to-go cups that I purchased from the tribe earlier who was selling wares."

"I know, right!" said Constantine. "And look how they seem like regular communion cups, but they are not! They are like our Allan Guth robes, but cups that expand forever."

"You gotta love it!" laughed Mirian. "We can pour so much of the blood in here and never fill it up!" quietly laughed Mirian.

"You know that is not my blood, don't you?" said Advocate.

"Well, not if you ask the Blacks," laughed Constantine.

"Yeah," said Mirian. "They covered themselves in it during the epidemics."

"Now, wait just a minute," Malcolm said as he felt the tension rising.

"Well," responded Mirian, "if you don't believe me, go down to the floor of Sardis and ask some of them."

"Pence," chimed in Constantine, "you can ask thousands of them for they died just like the COVID deniers, for all the good the 'blood' did for them." King Menelik quietly chuckled, for he did not like Blacks' ignorance of their borrowed God and thought the pun was humorous. Mirian started laughing hard and stomped his feet like the African Americans he enjoyed imitating.

"Now, wait one damn minute," shouted King Martin. "What are we going to do about these Rednecks? They, as a whole, mock everything the Advocate stands for, and you two are always drunk or high!"

"Hey, now!" Mirian responded to Martin. "You sound like those Black grandmothers who come here crying, 'oh my baby; he smokin' those tweeds.' And all the while, the White grandmother is encouraging the sale of pharmaceuticals, making billions in the process!"

"Yeah, the bad ones like opioids," Constantine responded.

"All the way to the carlsontucking bank!" laughed Mirian.

"Damn you Romans!" shouted King Martin.

"Shhhhh," said Queen Makeda, who is King in Heaven. The two Bro Kings, Constantine and Mirian, smiled, sank into their thrones, and sipped the wine like tea brewed by Wendy Williams and stirred by her own hand. Maurice the Saint smiled and thought better of the kings. After all, the General was no fan of Black Culture because he felt they cared nothing for him or his sacrifice for Christianity.

"King Malcolm?" Queen Makeda said, prompting Malcolm to take the reigns of the meeting.

"This is what we know," said King Malcolm. "The Rednecks have blacked out Heaven's eyes, for we can no longer see what is happening on Earth. With their foolish act of January 6th earlier this year, the insurrectionists…"

"Rednecks!" interrupted King Martin. "They are carlsontucking Rednecks!"

"That's what I said," responded King Malcolm, who remained cooler than a polar bear's toenails. "The Rednecks, as I have said, have broken the Seals of Lankford, who placed the seals over Washington, D.C so that Heaven may always keep an eye on the country, and therefore, the world's movement and development of White Phuckery, the old-timey magic of the Crackers. Since they have broken the seals, it is as if the entire

113

continent was Dubai, which no Paradise, angel, nor immortal has ever been able to see from the astral plane."

King Malcolm went on.

"We also know that since then, the days of Dark Brandon, the withering son of the half-breed Orisha, Barracka Flacka O'beezy, has covered the world with madness, for he toys with the Rednecks at his peril. He makes a firm decision about nothing until it's too late, and America is like a dog chasing its tail. That is if the dog's tail was a cache of C4. Putini has invaded Ukraine, and from what I understand from Martin's Celestial concubine, it was at the behest of the Wrath Writer, the Carnivorous Alchemist, among other things."

"Why have you let this little Negro run amok," King Martin sternly asked the Advocate. The Advocate sighed and said nothing.

"Now, Brotha," interrupted Malcolm. "You need to chill for a moment. There's time for us to discuss all."

"What happened to 'by any means necessary?" Martin quipped.

"It is the 'means' we now discover, Brotha, by which means we have available. You know, getting shot, I think, has done more to your soul and patience, than your body," King Malcolm responded.

"Well," interjected the Advocate. "It is not easy for martyrs to turn the other cheek in the Second Life. Some scars fester in the soul long after rigor mortis has riddled the earthly flesh. Even now, the coins about my hand itch, and when they do, I often think of my crucifixion."

"This is true," responded King Menelik.

"Pence! My head still hurts," sighed Martin.

"Let's continue," said Queen Makeda.

"Now, Ninth Born," said King Malcolm, "while we spoke earlier…"

"You mean, while planning your orgy," Queen Makeda could not help but interject.

"Why, Queen Sheba," King Malcolm responded as he kept his composure. He then winked at Robert the Deuce, in which the king of the Alphabet people threw up his two fingers as if she was swearing an oath to pussy, and smiled.

"If we cannot see the Earth," responded the Advocate, "then maybe, Queen Makeda, you can just listen in and tell us what's going on down there since your hearing is like the Ether, which has a better range than 100G." General Maurice smirked as General Tariq hid his face from embarrassment. King Robert the Deuce laughed hysterically.

"Yeah, what's up with the orgies?" Constantine and Mirian asked simultaneously.

"No need to be bashful," responded the Queen. "This is Heaven, and we are allowed to live out our ideals of heavenly happiness. I, too, took part in the orgies until the algorithms kept sending me seventy-two virgins. Who the Alabama (Hell) want to be deep-rodded by the souls of virgin men? I have no heavenly idea." Then the Queen threw a skull of a CIA agent at the head of Mark Dorsey, the creator of the social media platform, Soul Snatch, who cried and crawled behind King Ataris's throne. Everyone laughed, for they all hated the platform they deemed the abyss's spirit in digital form.

"Now that we've all enjoyed a good laugh at this servant of Mammon's expense," said Queen Sheba, "please, King Malcolm, continue on." And Malcolm continued.

"As I was saying, we now know that the Ether no longer flows from the Ether Domain, the domain of the Duke, who is the keeper of the holy spirit. It doesn't matter how much of the AllGod's plant, the God Bush, we smoke; we cannot tap into the Ether. We have no way of communicating with the great smoke golem, who is the Duke and the embodiment of the holy spirit. He will not intervene on Heaven's behalf unless the AllGod is present or commands. So we have no way of communing through the holy spirit.

We've spoken to the souls of many Christian women, and as they tell it, the chickens have come home to roost. The worst of the Cracker Nation, the Nationalists, have sunk into every government. For every strong man at the head of these snakes, their bodies are straw men. The not-so Supreme Court of the Native American's stolen land gears itself to ban abortion across the board, giving no power or quarter to mortal women, Earth godlings who are the masters of birth, life, and their bodies."

"It's what happens when White men with no principles have power," spoke King Robert. "Did you not leave the Georgia Guidestones to reference in such times?"

"Yes, but he used a racist," General Tariq quickly said and lowered his head as the Advocate stared. Then King Ataris spoke in his Ebonic language, and the Advocate responded.

"Well, King Ataris, yes," responded the Advocate. "But, find a stone cutter..."

"... that's not racist, we know!" Queen Makeda responded. "But out of all places, you chose Georgia. I believe the Marines would say that has 'good decision, bad judgment' written all over it," responded Queen Makeda. "And for the blood of Christ! Please continue, Malcolm." Malcolm continued as Constantine passed his cup to the Queen, which she attempted to down out of frustration. Constantine then motioned for the cup to return, which he did not receive.

"And finally," King Malcolm said, "we know that you have one of the Twelve Bondless Timepieces of Hodgkins. We understand that the immortal Anthony Hodgkins created the timepieces. However, we know not for what or whom. Although considering the request, it would have to come from one of the Supreme Beings, either Death or Evil, the Collective, if not the AllGod, who is the light. Then Malcolm leaned to the edge of his throne and said:

"Warlord of Warlords, could you show us the timepiece you have in your possession?"

From within his Alan Guth robe of infinite space, Ninth Born pulled out the sixth timepiece of Anthony Hodgkins, the Skeleton Key. The Skeleton Key, by its design, counts down to the exact moment in time that the dead flesh of soulless corpses swim through the oceans, fly about the air, and walk upon this Earth with complete thought, eyes with empty glare. They are the soulless bodies of those called the Living Shook, But only one soul in that room knew of this information.

"I know not what this timepiece does or who it is meant for," said the Advocate. "The Archangel Prevail gave me this the exact moment after my classification. He knew not what the timepiece does either, but my father left instructions for Prevail to place it in my care. However, it has been counting down to midnight in my possession, which is thousands of years. According to the Skeleton Key, twilight will be upon us soon."

"The Cracker Books! The Cracker Books! For the love of the AllGod Almighty, let us discuss the destruction of the Cracker Books!" repeatedly shouted King Martin.

"So we have come to it," said Lord Sheba, Makeda the Favored. "What shall we do about the talking books and the rest of these matters?" The room became as quiet as the abyss as they all stared upon the face of the Advocate.

"If I may," the Advocate said after a long silence befell the room, "I would like to question Lana De Rothchill, this Celestial of Martin's, for I do not feel that she is here out of her own fruition nor Martin's."

"What do you mean?" grumbled Martin. "My Howley is legendary in these streets." Martin then motioned his hand above his head. The court of Martin, which numbered three thousand, parted, and the Celestial, Lana De Rothchill, who was in the allure of a well-shaped Ukranian woman, covered in robes and of Turkish descent, walked to the front and stood beside Martin's throne. She then bowed.

"Why are you here, Celestial?" asked the Advocate. Lana looked around the court at all the kings and then smiled as she placed her hand on Martin's shoulder.

"I'm here because Martin's Howley is legendary on these holy streets," Lana said, mocking the Advocate. The Advocate's eyes flared, for he was not pleased. But, Rothchill quickly contrived. "But, I am also here at the behest of Carnegie Black, the Wrath Writer, and the Lord of Nabu."

"To what end?" asked Ninth Born in reply. Lana answered:

"To bear witness on behalf of the Lord of Nabu, to the magnificence of the AllGod's power."

"What do you mean?" asked King Brusilia in a deep, low, and smooth voice like Barry White, if his dick could talk. "Bear witness to an AllGod miracle or to the AllGod, himself?"

"Bear witness to the Roman who shares the AllGod's word; by fulfilling this oath, We take notice of the soldier of the Lord."

"Finally!" said General Maurice. "You don't know how long this pence has been stirring around this old soul's noggin."

"Maurice, what's this business you speak of?" asked the

Advocate. "Are you truly the agent of Carnegie within my house?"

"Relax!" said General Maurice the Saint. "I'm not two timing my warlords, Warlord of Warlords." Maurice lit Lana, switching out the dirty weed for the God Bush, and then lit the pipe, which sparked like fire and let loose a thick cloud of vibrant green. His eyes turned bright purple as his face gleamed. Then the Theban reached over the breastplate of his golden armor and into the center of his chest. He pulled out from within his being the first of the Twelve Timepieces of Hodgkins, the Cosmic Clock, the Flava Flav Watch.

Constantine sunk in his chair and moaned, for the timepiece radiated the AllGod's spiritual pressure that few could withstand. Ataris was struck motionless. The light that flickered in his typeball eye went dim like Ron "Sugar Boots" DeSantis when he can't pussy-fuss his way out of the question. His head slumped over.

Every king's court, some like Ataris, numbered in the tens of thousands. Like all the kings of the Thirty-Sixth Chamber, Ataris placed his closest Council behind his throne.

Behind Ataris were the many souls of urban models like Elkis the Stallion, whose giant, perfect ass had broken the internet well before the curse of social media began. These gorgeous women had earned a place in Ataris's digital Paradise. They are called Alencar's media muses – in the digital plane of Ataris, which floated above his head like a cube. All the courts fell flat on the floor from the spiritual pressure. But the Alencars fell to their knees and faces leaving their asses up and their elbows down before them. Sojourner leaned against the wall as the intense weight fell upon her and struck her hard. Queen Sheba and King Martin held their heads in their hands, and then Sheba screamed. "Put it back in! Please put it back in!"

"Sorry there, your highnesses," Maurice responded. Maurice stood as relaxed as the Advocate, for the timepiece bore tremendous pressure upon his soul. "I haven't had this thing for that long, but it is like the spirit of Roscoe Dash with the AllGod's power; the timepiece is 'all the way turnt up.'"

Then General Maurice squeezed the chained device, and the spiritual pressure within the room receded. King Mirian crawled back into his chair because the AllGod's power "had him on the floor like Luda." The typeball in Ataris, The Technite's, eye started to glow again. And in his language, he asked his fellow kings what the technical tuck!

"It is like a power that I have never felt before," said King Brusilia, who merely leaned over on his throne, for he had the power of two mighty souls.

"That is a glimpse of the AllGod's power, your majesties, and it is apparent that none of you have ever been in his presence before," said Maurice as he held the timepiece out in his hand. The Cosmic Clock then rose into the air, centering itself in the center of the exposed chain. Then the chain began to rotate clockwise as the timepiece, carved with an arrow outside its metal case, turned in the opposite direction.

"I'd thought the lot of you would have met him when he came back for the Blues King homecoming," Maurice pondered.

The Advocate, fighting the bitterness of Maurice's admission, turned toward the Roman General and said. "Blues, the King of Strings, was a warrior like no other in the eyes of my father and was dear to his heart. The Blues King's notes are as sweet and crucial to time as Gabriel's horn. My father considered the String King prestigious, more so than the Seraphim and all that he made like the angels who were the first to breathe the breath of life. Though millions of souls attended the parade, ceremony, and banquet in the tune maker's honor, it would be considered a close-door event by Heaven's standards. Not many this low below Heaven's wealth would have stood and remembered his coming and passing."

"You don't say?" pondered Maurice as his eyes still glowed purple from the cosmic device's spiritual power. "Well, I didn't think so in the first place: you kings amuse me. But, not many can stand in the ALFAMAK's presence, I would imagine. I could not, for I was torn apart and later put back together by Carnegie Black, though the AllGod left him the twelfth timepiece, the watch called the Happiest Hour. The clock in Carnivorous' possession reverses the ruin of souls and makes the undone whole again.

"But still, Carnegie required time and other tools within his control to complete my reform. And then he sealed me so I could not tell what transpired until the appropriate time.

"But, let us be like Tiesto and get down to business, shall we? Heaven and its councils do not have even a night to grasp and understand this. You will have much work to do, Advocate, on top of completing the Mass Choir. But you will need help, and time is waning. And, after so long, I am tired of carrying this power-draining gadget.

"But now all of Heaven bears witness and is authorized to accept this possession as an oath fulfilled." Maurice pointed to the Cosmic Clock, like a Flava Flav Watch, and a clairvoyant voice came from the timepiece and echoed through the Chamber. The vocals emitted had prestige and carried authority like the melody of Lord Rakim, who made a joyous clap upon the world.

"Hear thy vessel's voice and let the vibe hit like fire from the altar of rejoice.

"Heed the commands of the AllGod, for the soldier now expresses his desire."

King Brusilia whispered to King Robert, "Talking books and now fancy, talking watches. What will the Heavens think of next? Medical plans that cover 100% birth control?"

Still, in awe of the Cosmic Clock, King Robert whispered, "Uh-uh, that's old and done. See, the AllGod works miracles, but Barracka Flacka O'beezy does the health care."

"Wow! That is intense, right?" General Maurice grinned. "Musa, do you still wish to tell me more about the AllGod."

"Musa fell to his knees and stared at the purple glowing timepiece with amazement in his eyes and a joyful look upon his face.

"It is an honor to be in the presence of the AllGod's power," General Tariq said with tears streaming down his face. "May the truly powerful be praised. My friend, do not hesitate further to do as AllGod has commanded. Please, perform the ALFAMAK, the Father of All Mankind's, business, and will."

"This timepiece is the Cosmic Clock, the Flava Flav," spoke General Maurice as the watch levitated while circling him. "It is the first in the order of the Twelve Bondless Timepieces the immortal Anthony Hodgkins assembled, although being the last watch in the series he produced. Each of the Twelve accounts for significant happenings within eternity, events considered universe-altering. Individually or paired with its sister watches, the ancient devices count down to the destruction of the holy seals, many on Earth, that keep the AllGod's One Reality in place.

"Once made, the watch foretold the rise of the half-breed spirit, the lowly Magada Gaga, the Covfefe, Demitri 'Grift' Griffington, III. It spoke of the Magada destiny, which was to consume the lost power of Mammon and sit atop America's highest pole, gripping the flag of Betsie like a humping dog upon a meaty bone. It foretold the destruction of Mammon and the slaying of Shub-Niggurath and the Archangel Samuel by the Black Knights of the Riviera at the time of Hurricane Michael. It told of Putini's delusion, exploitation of Russia, and Ukraine's rise, which laid the dictator low.

"The timepiece told of the coupling between the White and Christian Nationalists and the Cracker Nation with the Neanderthals. It told of the corrupted who now all worship Odin instead of Mammon, the Money God, who is now dead. And it predicted the wrath of the Dark Alchemists of Nabu, the Black Knights, who would not rise in time unless provoked in death.

"Hodgkins was not bound by the forward flow of time but transversed eternity in his life span, from the end of time back to the beginning. At the end of eternity, the noose of time will be no more, for there will be a consumption of the stars and the planets by Laniakea, the AllGod in empyrean form. And the remaining energy outside the Advocate's established Paradise will be sucked up by Laniakea, and the universe outside the astral plane will die.

"But, as this universe's energy was drawn back into oblivion by the AllGod, for this has already occurred, Hodgkins knelt before the AllGod's Throne that sits at the tip of Laniakea's hummingbird-like beak. Anthony wept before the Light of Laniakea as she drew in all the universe's remaining energy. And when the AllGod asked Lord Anthony how oblivion came to give so quickly, the actor spoke to the Divine One. Lord Anthony, the immortal, confessed to AllGod what transpired on Earth from the year 2016 to the year 2030. He conveyed all ruin that came to pass. He explained the actions of the Rednecks and all they had planned with Q'Nah Nah, the planet Q, and the oaths they broke by her trickery and mastery of social media. Anthony told the AllFather the laws of Heaven and Earth that the insurrectionists had shredded. He told him of the broken seals, the strong men about every nation like crazed gerbils within a wheel. He spoke to the AllFather and said that the Rednecks had aligned Heaven with Earth, which sped up the end of times."

Then Maurice beckoned the Advocate to pull out the Skeleton Key, which he did

When the Advocate presented the Skeleton Key timepiece before the General, the watch raised and drifted into the middle of the chain surrounding the Cosmic Clock and began to move like the minute hand of a clock and rotated backward to midnight.

"We are less than a mortal day away from midnight," professed the Theban, "which means war is imminent with the Living Shook, the soulless bodies of those affected by the Requiem Virus. And also, based on what the Book of Abbott has unwittingly confessed, the Neanderthals will enter this plane with the Living Shook in an attempt to retrieve Odin's eye, which powers Sardis. A portion of the Forever War is upon us and it will determine the establishment of the AllSavior Paradise and the Crackers' domination."

"Tariq," the Advocate said as he turned to the General. "Where was Abbott's book when you found it?"

"I found it laughing as it hovered above Abbott's burnout corpse," Tariq said. "I apologize for not mentioning this before, but I confess that I was overwhelmed by the phenomenon of the talking books. But yes. The book hovered above the mangled corpse of what I assumed was its actual body. It was cursing the body."

"Well," said Ninth Born. "That is confirmation of the Living

Shook being in this plane. However, I am unsure how the flesh of any soul who wasn't preordained entered the House of Sardis."

"Advocate," said Tariq. We must acknowledge that Q'Nah is up to her tricks with the minds of the Wafer and weak."

"About that," Lana Rothchill chimed in. "Fault not Q, the manifestation of the Earth, for she is sick with a disease. She can no longer bear what the world has done to her. Q has made deals with the Black Knights and the Cracker Nation to bring this moment of the Forever War to Heaven's door. If the Nationalists caused the breaking of time and have both the Earth and Heaven cosmically aligned, chaos is out of order, and all that Hodgkins assembled would be for naught. But, if this skirmish of the Forever War is fought and won in the astral plane and not on Earth, it is a war in Heaven. Thus the destruction of the National resurrectionists is then permitted with no punishment of the victor. Therefore, no violations of the AllGod's have occurred."

"Maurice, is this the idea presented to you by my father?" asked the Advocate.

"No, Warlord," said Maurice as he commanded the timepieces, which were still joined, out of the House of Sardis. "The Carnivore's plan has brought us to this moment. He told me to send the two timepieces out of the House of Sardis just as I have done. It was he who told me to swear allegiance to you and stand with you until you dismissed me. But it was the AllGod's order that he followed. Everything that has transpired here at this moment is all part of a plan that the Carnivorous Alchemist came up with after Hodgkins explained the events that led to the Cracker Nation's false reality. The AllGod granted him plenty of latitudes."

"He has met my father?" angrily asked the Advocate.

"Well, I wouldn't know, my Lord, for I was in pieces," stated

General Maurice. "So, I think that is a story for another day. One you should hear from the Carnivore's mouth, so to speak. And if we do this right, all of us, you will get your wish of battle and mayhem sooner rather than later! You will not have to wait for the action of the Forever War to begin to wreck pence and wreak havoc upon the wicked and Wafery."

King Martin stood up, threw a fist in the air, and said, "All my damn afterlife, I have been praying to the AllFather, the AllMighty, for this moment! I've hoped to sweet Heaven for an opportunity to be upon a fair footing with Christian Nationalists so that I can whoop the monkey-Gaetz of some Crackers – oh, thank you, AllLord. I've watched their ignorant selves, wondering through Sardis, gradually walking their funky Gaetz down to the pit of the Confederacy like it's just another Cracker holiday! Hallelujah! And when very few of them receive salvation, they walk about Heaven's first and second floor like they own the place. But the celebration is all mine now, for you, Advocate, must achieve your dreams and put some holes in some fools who think they can slap box with Heaven. That isn't right! These fools don't know the gentrifiers of the Earth are the hired help in all the spiritual places, especially in Heaven."

Then Ataris hovered above his throne, glowing green all over, and, in his Ebonics AI language, said:

"Tuck these tuckin' calrsontuckers, they tuckin' tucked! We should meet these bucks in battle wherever they lay at, wherever they stay at, for real for real, and rat-ta-tat-tat the Mitches like yeah-yeah-yeah, Mitches, you knew the Advocate would return. You knew he would be back! So why yo' Mitch-Gaetz flex and act like that? The wicked: plow-boom-pow, dead, dead, dead! Do you know what I mean?"

Maurice became aroused and said, "I know precisely what

the tuck you mean. I didn't understand a word, but I heard you, my sentient brother. You speak from the soul, and I'm with it one hundred. Advocate, you should listen to the Automaton. He makes an excellent point. A little Slaughter Gang now removes some Crackers from the board who still deal in White Phuckery, that old-timey magic. The same Mitch-Gaetz Magic that Heaven thought to destroy long ago. White Nationalists and Christian fanatics, all fascists. Neanderthals. I overheard something about gremlins – tuck them too. AllLord, there are so many birds and so many stones, all within the AllGod's plan. We should be like smokey and take advantage."

The Advocate's eyes wandered around the Chamber, which had its walls raised.

He searched through the souls of all in his company. And as he starred at each soul, gathering the measure and wisdom of his advice, he rubbed the flesh around the coins on his hand and thought about the suffering of the Earth Godling, who is womankind, and the woes of Q, the planet, dying. He thought of how much the Rednecks have fucked up in the last millennium. He thought about the bashing of Robert's people. He thought about the followers of Q and how she must hate them. He thought of how much he disliked Texas and became furious.

"Yes! We are going to get at them, son!" shouted the Advocate.

"Yeahhhh!" screamed Maurice. "How do you want to go about it? Raise the alarms. Rally the battalions of angels. Or should we start spearing tuckers with tucked-up haircuts and carrying tiki torches?"

"No, no," the Advocate replied. "For this to work, we must let them believe that they are in control so that them Mitches don't chicken out. What I know about insurrectionists is that they would tuck up a free lunch if you let them. Let them carry out their ridiculous plans, thinking the details are of their design. When the timing is right, I will command the mortal forces of the Kingdom of Heaven against the Wafers and all that would damn the world to Alabama! Leave the angels out, for they will not recognize this as war, nor should they. The White souls on levels one and two pull some crap just about every other day, and the angels barely flinch any more. Plus, I am only authorized to command them when I return to Earth. So, let us enjoy this moment that I test out the mantel of 'Warlord of Warlords'."

Then Lord Tariq said, "Should I recall Juice Li?"

"Yes!" replied the Advocate. "That is an excellent idea, for I know he craves battle as my Divine Guard, just as much as I. Retrieve him from the lower levels, but tell him nothing of what we discuss."

Then Queen Makeda said, "Then, tell no one! Only those present should be aware of the Cracker Mitches' moves. Tell not an angel. Tell not Musa, your other Divine Aide, for he overreacts and would bring forth his horde. Tell not a soul outside these raised walls, although I know Andre LaShay is listening with his noisy Gaetz."

"I can't lie,' shouted Andre directly outside the wall. "Yeah, I was listenin'. That's true. You got me."

"Tell no one, Andre," Queen Sheba replied.

"Nah, Nah," said Andre. "I never tell people's secrets. I sure don't."

So, as Sojourner lowered the walls to the Thirty-Sixth Chamber, the kings resumed praising the Judgment of the throne. King Constantine poured Queen Sheba another cup of wine and toasted her and King Mirian on the war to come. King Malcolm put one finger on his face and sat back on his throne. King Martin laughed like a schoolgirl, for he was pleased. As a General of the Mortal Guard, Sojourner began to make arrangements for the fortification of Heaven's parameter. Tariq was to summon Juice Li without causing alarm. And so, the generals accompanied one another as they traveled to the lowest level of Heaven.

With the walls of the Thirty-Sixth Chamber lowered, the Advocate was free to walk to the edge of the platform. He stared down upon his station in deep contemplation. He smiled and thought of all that had transpired. As he touched the coin upon his hand to transport himself in a bolt of lightning, he turned around and smiled at Queen Sheba. She smiled back and quoted the Testament of Drake: "What a time to be alive, indeed."

And then, like smoke, the Advocate was gone.

Act Six

The Order of Business in Heaven

As the Advocate and Governor Musa looked upon the swarm of millions of souls scattered before them, a state of bewilderment fell upon the House of Sardis. There were many souls of Rednecks hovering, standing, and complaining before the Advocate's station in varying degrees of anger and anxiety, pushing and shoving their way past souls who had been there for ages. From what I understand, Redneck or not, it is quite normal for a newly arrived soul to be confused by the breathtaking yet terrifying surroundings.

At this moment in eternity, the *Requiem Virus* has ravaged the planet Earth, and many souls arrive in Heaven from the year 2021, around the fall, I do believe. It is the 6,052nd year in the Kingdom of Heaven, which lies in the astral plane, just like most spiritual kingdoms. At Heaven's gates, the victims of the virus impatiently wait, like all other souls, for trial. And it is the Advocate, the AllSavior, who is not only the soul's co-counsel and defender before the AllFather, but also presides over the Court of Supreme Judgment in the House of Sardis, where the First Life of gentile – non Jewish – Christian souls are judged.

Know that time functions differently within all the AllGod's planetary creations, as you may be aware, but especially those star systems located in the astral plane where all spiritual realms reside. A planet that exists in the physical world is measured in the frame of twenty-four hours and will slow down or speed up it's counter clockwise rotation according to its specific gravitational pull, as the AllGod designed. However, in the astral plane, he made it so that time is displaced significantly by the solar system's opposing rotation, much like Venus, meaning that in the astral plane, planets rotate clockwise, opposite the flow of time. There, in the astral plane, lies immortality. Or Venus, depending how you look at it.

In the beginning, the astral plane was an empty abyss just as the Trap – the ultimate void – before the megaverse was seeded and grown. But, over an eternity of experimenting with the science of creation known as Chaos Alchemy, which births all stars, the AllGod placed many creatures and calamities, which are living curses, inside the metaphysical plane. A plane completely outside the noose that is time. Know that the planets and stars within the astral plane were placed there by the AllGod so that the spiritual realm may grow and that souls, evil or righteous, will always have a home or a cell to continue to roam. And, now, we come to it! At Heaven's gates, non-Jewish Christian souls gather in numbers more remarkable than the Kingdom of Heaven has ever seen.

Sara Lynn Lee Barlow, a White woman from Wewahitchka, Florida, hovered just below the right shoulder of the Advocate, becoming more corporeal as the moments passed. Sara was fifty-three years old when she died on the Earth in 2021 and appeared before the Throne of Judgment shortly after.

Now, the Court of Judgment and all those to be judged gathered in the fifth great Hall of the Kingdom of Heaven called the *House of Sardis*, which sits just outside the thirteenth gate; that particular gate is called Addisu's *Offspring*. In the House of Sardis, as in all Houses of the AllGod, lies a Throne of Purpose.

But, in the House of Sardis, which was a house of justice, sat the Throne of Judgment. And it was purely location that made the House of Sardis the ideal place for the judgment of non-Chosen souls – not directly descended from Abraham – as it is the most direct passage to the cursed realm of the Confederacy, the Confederacy of Hell. And only the souls of the adopted children of Abraham, those souls claimed by the First Life of the Advocate, stood before it.

One should remember that Hell, or simply the Confederacy of Hell, is a union of the supernatural and the ordinary, Earth-located states that focuses on the fear and rage of the human condition. The Confederacy of Hell is in direct opposition to all that is righteous by the AllGod's design, as it always has been. Therefore, passages that connect to wicked places must also lead to heavenly ones from the living world. Nine gates connect Heaven and Hell to Earth in spiritual travel, but only one connects Heaven directly to Hell. Three join the Confederacy to the sorrowed territory of Alabama where the Gnome King – Beauregard Jeffers – resides, two to the Redneck Riviera where supernatural spirits, spiritual warlords and the cowards of life run to hide. Three more gates that reach up from the depths of Hell to chain misery to where men, dead in the eyes of Heaven live and dwell. But, it is the gate that lies in Sardis that connects Heaven to the Confederacy, and it is one-directional; a trash chute for the most pencient (shit like) souls and the demon spirits that torment men.

As Sara stood next to the Advocate, her soul began to materialize, or appear, in the same physical image as when she had died, which she felt was her prime. When Sara was alive, she was a vibrant vanilla shake with more curves than breaks. Her cheeks were rosy. She had a phat apple bottom and hips to match, and she had that natural tan that Rednecks produce when they have had just the right amount of sun or light like an easy-bake oven; some mortal's skin is so fragile. But, no! No spray tan, "fake ass African in a can" for Sara. In no way did she believe that she ever in life subscribed to that fake shit.

Sara was a woman who lived her life believing she had a fair moral compass.

She was a person who understood bullshit when she heard it. Yes. In life, she had more pleasant days than not. And being the whimsical type of broad that she was, she chose to materialize in her favorite blue iris fleece jacket, black cotton pants combination that she boosted from Marshalls in 2018, during the mayhem that occurred directly after Hurricane Michael struck the Riviera. Such comfortable attire, indeed.

Now, Sara, or her soul, I should say, could not find the words to speak, despite the lack of trying. She looked upon the fiery gleam from the Advocate's face, which brightened the brow of his braided black and silver hair of wool and fiery eyes that, when gazed upon by Sara, shook her to the core of her soul. She knew, at once, that he was *the Great Redeemer, the AllGod's begotten son born to Chosen Ones, and also the children of Menelik, who are the children of Sheba, who are the children of Addisu.*

Because of that lineage, to Sara, the Advocate was much darker in complexion than she had expected. So sexy, powerful, and dignified, Sara thought to herself which made her weep in all places as her soul formed. But, with all the energy of her being that she could muster, she could not say the Advocate's holy name. She hadn't the command of the soul just yet.

Behind Sara was Rupert Emilio Portman, the Texan, a sixty-six-year-old Crackerish congressman from the enormously backward realm of Texas, an energy-abusing region located in the

Americas of Earth. Rupert was hung upon a Texas courthouse when the U.S. currency lost its place as Earth's reserve currency in 2030. But, unlike Sara, Rupert became corporeal instantly as he was delivered to Heaven.

Behind the Texan, that privileged motherfucker, was D'jon Hardgrove, a fifty-four-year-old Black Detroit bus driver who died at the hands of a woman suffering from the Requiem Virus in 2021. He was strangled by the woman he called a nasty ass bitch when she did not cover her mouth after coughing. The six foot, Neanderthal-sized woman strangled him for it. Unfortunately, D'jon was driving at the time.

And behind that gentle giant were millions of other souls arriving at the Gate of Judgment, each at different moments of eternity and from many different places on Earth, at their predetermined position in line and death. It is important to note that only planets that have achieved rebirth – planetary judgment – are aligned directly with the timeline of Heaven. So, it is unusual in Heaven for the present to supersede the past. But, there stood at the gates of eternal life many. Millions of souls that perished during that tragic ass year on Earth came to Heaven's Hall, some directly from 2021 and others from 2030, still remarkably close to the year they died.

But, the Advocate has always made ill-fated times work to his benefit. He could feel the end of times drawing near. He had hidden hopes that the noose could once and for all tighten no more and that his return to Earth would be upon him. But, as he knew his father's mind and the truths that General Maurice displayed before the kings, all he felt was geared to this one battle brewing before Heaven's gates. A battle with the Crimson Dead, the once loyal to his word, now beholden to Odin and mayhem.

Nevertheless, Ninth Born made up his mind to use the events

laid before him and prevail. And so, in his plans, he sought to finish filling the ranks of Heaven's one million-member choir. It has 856,000 excellent, boisterous souls in eternity and requires 144,000 more. It was his father's work that weighed heavily on his mind.

"Be patient, my child," the Advocate said to the strawberry blonde Redneck named Sara, who was still attempting to speak.

"And, I like your hair," he added, smiling at the woman that died in her prime. She had a reddish tent to her hair that stretched down to the bottom of her curvature, making her look as fun as a strawberry red Lamborghini. The Advocate was very fond of this type of woman when he walked the Earth in his First Life. He would never say aloud unless provoked, but he found a boring bitch nearest to death.

"It works for you," the Advocated continued as he looked past her projection and into her decisions and life events that connected her birth to her death, like the roots of a sprouting evergreen.

"Life in the flesh is the most complex," Ninth Born said while viewing the inevitable pitfalls that plague the mortal's soul. "It is as if every step concerning love, trust, and self-esteem for a human being, especially that of a woman, was a stumbling affair in the most predatory jungle. Your life, like so many, appears as if the Earth, Q'Nah Nah herself, laid forth a labyrinth of unavoidable missteps and misled deeds."

"Tell me," the Advocate requested. "On Earth, do you not yet have a free college or higher-education type of social system in your day and time? Or, are White men still hoarding words, numbers and parchment as if they created them in the first place?"

135

Sara became flustered and did not understand the barrage of questions. She systematically reviewed every decision of her life that she felt to be a misstep in judgment. Sardis was on her side in this matter, for clarity is the order of that great house in Heaven. Truth is even more blaring when standing before the Advocate, as clarity is his aura and is forever present in his face.

"Mmm..." the Advocate murmured as he looked into Sara's eyes to scan her life, words, and earthly deeds. As he reviewed her soul, the Advocate rubbed his hands together up and down, left and right. Whenever he rubbed his hands intensely, the coins upon his palms would produce a sound similar to one thousand chimes or four thousand harmonic pans. Lightning would accompany this action, offering many bright flashes of colorful light. The sound frightened Sara so much that she assumed the frightening sound was appropriate for her judgment and did not bold well for her case.

And, at that moment within the House of Sardis, Sara struggled in the presence of great fear.

Act Seven

Clarity in the House of Sardis

As the lightning struck and the thunder rang out all around the House of Sardis, the Advocate analyzed Sara's First Life. He laughed at some moments of her life, shook his head at many others, and was frustrated. But, the Great Counselor smirked at the many times Sara refused to take shit from men. He understood Sara's many compromises as a woman under Crackerish rule. And the Advocate smiled as she loved rainy days as much as he did, for those were the days he enjoyed most while on Earth.

In particular, he loved the constant rainfalls of the Redneck Riviera from which Sara came. He did not have such an opportunity for rain while he was on the plains of Utah, where he spent most of his remaining time on Earth. But, that was in the early days after his resurrection. He was bound there for a while ministering to Moroni's people and many Native American tribes in that moistureless land. What few years he spent in the panhandle, prior to letting Dat Nigga 536 loose upon the Earth, he had a bitchin' good time, from what I understand.

But, when the Advocate was on Earth, he was fond of women with Sara's nature as he enjoyed conversations with those who did not waste his time with bullshit and kept it fucking real. Sara was feisty when dealing with the truth. The Advocate thought that to be a magnificent characteristic as it was what he enjoyed most about his bottom-dollar chic, Meeka Magdala, an African woman of wealth from the Sea of Galilee.

(B*ottom-dollar chic*: A woman you can count on through bad times and worse.

One may consider this woman a wife even though not legally married.)

Yes! The Advocate is forever a lover of truth and clearly understands the One Reality that his father, the AllGod, wields. But, because man is greedy and clumsy as carlsontucker, Heaven recognizes the amateurism of White man's attempt at controlling reality. The algorithms of Mormon Law, which now manages the kingdom, accounts for earthly debacles. There have been many reconstructions of Heaven's rules before due to the Advocate, who is the AllGod's earthly sacrifice. And as far as Advocate was concerned, he profoundly loved honest conversations which he found only resulted from discussions with one kind of human: a seasoned woman.

(Tuck: meaningless replacement for the curse word fuck. "–tucking" is an alternative for the word "fucking". Derived from the name of the Weasel News Commentator, Carlson 'Fucker' Tucker, III, who is hated by all of the astral plane and every immortal who has heard of his pencetucking name.)

(*Pence*: Shit. Manure. Sometimes bitch. A male mothering motherfucker. A person who is an indecisive weakling whose only decisiveness is to hold progress or progressive people back. People who hover over other people or make decisions without authority.

A disliked stepparent with no kids of their own but insists that they are knowledgeable. A man that cowards to his wife, office, or duty as if it or she was his mother.)

"It seems that you've chosen the allure – the physical image – of your later years rather than your younger ones," the Advocate said as he laughed. Sara curled a nervous smile. In the Kingdom of Heaven, a Christian soul is at home and should only be as shameless as the animals. But, the strings that tether a soul to salvation also bind it to damnation. Consequently, it is not uncommon for a soul to feel the emotions it once felt in life, despite the clarity one receives in the House of Sardis. Some teeter to happiness. Some express everlasting sadness. Some poor sons of bitches meet the Advocate with the same piss and vinegar that soured their lives before their first deaths. But, as you know, regardless of the circumstances, humans are creatures of habit and will find themselves in the same predicaments in the afterlife as they once lived. I guess it is what it is, for, in the House of Sardis, the damned are also represented by the Advocate, and in that way, all will get their day.

"You are a woman who enjoyed her 'thickness,' I see," the Advocate said as Sara's deeds passed before his eyes like a tickertape spewing the naughtiness of her mind. The spiraling pillars of fire that lies, one each, in the iris of the Advocate's eyes, crackled like a campfire each time he saw a glimpse of Sara showing her ass – so to speak. Sara was certified a PAWG (Phat-Ass White Girl) during the annual Redneck Riviera event, the Panama City's 2010 Friday Fest, when she was forty-three. Although the Advocate did not condone lust, he knew that a woman had to shake her ass every once in a while, or the kitties turn into lions on the prowl.

"Well, you know," Sara said as she slowly began to speak. "I can talk!" she said, surprised that she had regained her voice. Now wholly corporeal, she felt reassured. But then Sara looked down at her shoes.

"Oh, pence! Oh, no!" she thought to herself. She quickly

scanned up and down the manifestation of her soul, from the left ankle bracelet to the stylish blouse. Suddenly Sara realized that she materialized before the Advocate in pence that she had boosted from Marshalls.

Sara quickly looked up at the Advocate and stared into the fiery pillars in his eyes. But then the Advocate sighed and smirked at Sara. Sara smiled back. Then Sara tilted her head down as she blushed a shade of red that would make a candy apple Lamborghini envious.

Ninth Born was amused by her behavior, and also returned with laughter. But, his mind is forever on his purpose and tasks at hand, and therefore, all the posturing with Sara just to cross-examine her soul began to wear his patience thin.

"Well, Governor Musa? The Rednecks? There are many of them and they are everywhere," the Advocate questioned with a great sigh, still reviewing Sara's life year after year. Sara's five-finger red bottom pumps hovered about four and a half feet above the emerald and diamond-encrusted floor, which allowed the Advocate to peer directly into the portals of the soul. Sara trembled a bit as she was shaken by the great height of the Advocate, and then she made no sound or twitch as she was then deep within the Advocate's gaze.

Now, Governor Musa was struck motionless just like Sara, not by paralysis of spirit but one of thought as he had new and growing concerns that overwhelmed him. Musa was standing to the left of the Advocate, facing the throne, when he started to sense an energy that he had not felt during his thousand years of servitude in Heaven. Ill-vibing energy it was. And Musa felt this peculiar power resonating from far off into the gaggle of souls gathered in the House of Sardis.

"Governor!" the Advocate sharply said before turning

toward Musa, who was perplexed by the masses of souls. The Governor, who then turned his body toward the Advocate half mannered, split his attention between Ninth Born, and the ill-vibing energy, like a burdened animal's hoof. The Advocate spoke.

"Musa! Please, say something? I'm reduced to advocating for souls one at a time instead of scanning their Books of Life for mass processing. I've been on this particular woman for what feels like forever." Then the Advocate, who now had his back toward Sara, pointed over his shoulder to a random, douchebag red hat wearing soul and said, "This Redneck soul can't sing, Musa. I'm sure of it." Then, as the Advocate began to go through his seamless robe, rumbling as if he had misplaced what he sought, he leaned into Musa and jokingly whispered:

"What the fluffy White phuckery is this, Musa? Out of all junctures in eternity, why stagnation at such an important moment?"

"Oh! Apologies," Musa whispered back with a slight laugh underneath his words recognizing Ninth Born's humor; he only joked when he wished to keep his inner peace. Musa, also acknowledging the Advocate's growing frustration, replied with promptness.

"Great Counselor. There is an explanation," Governor Musa said with some reluctance. Still, as soon as he began to address the Advocate, Musa refocused his attention on the energy vibrating through Sardis, which gave him great worry.

"God Sun, you don't feel that?" Musa asked the Advocate, but Ninth Born's attention was split as he struggled with the pocket dimensions within his seamless robe. Knowing what the Great Counselor sought, Musa reached into his own seamless robe of various silks, black, gold and purple, and pulled out a purple velvet pouch, similar to the Crown Royal bag of late. Musa opened the bag and pulled out a large pouch of God Bush, the sweetest carlsontucking marijuana, Father Strain, that he had already ground and prepared. He held the pinch in his fingers before the Advocate and said, "Messenger, present your pipe."

"Oh!" the Advocate said as he shifted his hand within his robe. He pulled his long-stemmed smoking pipe, Black Lazarus, from a more accessible point within the pocket dimension than the sticky icky he so desperately rambled to acquire.

"Thank you. For the Second Life of me, I can not find my goody bag of greatness inside this Alan Guth robe," the Advocate said in relief as Musa stuffed his pipe with the granules of the God Bush, the Father of all marijuana plants, that Musa, his Divine Aide, had on the ready.

"This buys you mere moments, Musa," said the Advocate. "We have a unique opportunity to complete at least a couple of my father's great works. We cannot stop since we've already started. We are now committed." He winked his right eye above the pipe's bowl, flickering flint that set the master strain ablaze. All through the House of Sardis, the fumes of Father Bush rolled high upon its jeweled floor like a tsunami's wave, blowing out its high rising doors, and across the cloud-covered hills of Heaven's gate. A rejuvenation of spirit and soul was about that sector of the astral plane in which Heaven resides.

There was a new calm about the place. And all were serene, the damned and dignified alike, except for Musa, who was still searching for energy that had no proper position in Sardis, and some of the caretakers of Sardis, who were snickering, for they knew this mood was temporary.

As the Advocate blew clouds of ganja that whipped like tangible winds, Musa grew more anxious. "Great counselor," he said again as he fiddled with the jeweled rings that covered every finger of his right hand, clicking the boggles against one another as he spoke. But, even that was another distraction for Musa, for the Governor was easily bewildered by matters that he felt required severe study. Musa struggled with great ventures, whether those of calamity or calmness. And it was his responsibility to draw the Books of Life from the souls so that the Advocate could reside over the quickest and most efficient judgments under Mormon Law.

"The Books of Life, Musa," the Advocate replied. "Maybe this mass gaggle tuck of souls would be less of a burden for the House of Sardis, I say more specifically, for you, Musa, if you would just take this step: retrieve the books, so we can get on with the primary business at hand." The Advocate returned his attention to Sara for he was prepared for war, and the inevitable outcome of Musa interacting with the talking Redneck books.

Act Eight

Karen Roars in Heaven

A mortal should know that as per the Supreme Being agreement between the Lord Death and the AllGod, all Christian souls – Jew or adopted – are escorted to Heaven by the Umvuni Ovuthiwe, the Reapers of the Dominion of Death. Before this moment in Heaven, Governor Musa would have pulled the Books of Life directly from each soul as they are delivered to Heaven, thousands at a time, regardless of the soul's particular years of Christian death. But never had Musa received millions at one time. Not even during the Plagues. Many souls go straight to Hell, many to Purgatory without review.

Now, after the time on Earth that the first "righteous vessels" rose as humans and walked upright from the wombs of the evolved beasts and were labeled "man," the Kingdom of Heaven was created and it decreed that the flesh would contain the Book of Life as well as the soul. After all, nothing about a mortal's First Life is more important than what a soul experienced and learned while living a righteous life.

As souls are sent from the Kingdom of Heaven to walk the Earth in various races of man, souls were also charged to keep and maintain strict diaries of their trials of life on Earth, for the AllGod knew after Cain was born that all those fucking books weren't coming back to Heaven as designed. This is the principal reason the Advocate sacrificed his First Life so that adopted souls and their Books of Life could also enter Heaven, for nothing makes for more excellent reading than variety. At least, to the AllGod.

But, at this moment, Governor Musa, whose head had, at the end of his First Life, rolled down the steps of a Damascus palace, hesitated. He once took a second-handed initiative by ordering the complete invasion of Hispania (Spain) in the name of the Umayyad Caliphate in the year 711. Still, because Musa lost his life due to that decision, the former Governor of the North African region, Ifriqiya, has been slow to act on any decision forthrightly, even in Heaven. And, since he usually drew the Books of Life from each soul one at a time, Governor Musa was not prepared for the urgency, nor did he have the confidence possessed by the Advocate amid this strange new energy.

"Great Counselor," Musa said cautiously as the Advocate's impatience began to show. "I would suggest that maybe it is best that we not be hasty in completing the Kingdom of Heaven's Mass Choir." Ninth Born whipped his head around in disbelief concerning what he was hearing. Musa averted his eyes and shrank beneath the Advocate's gaze. Then, with complete humility, Musa said: "Something is afoul in the kingdom and I believe it has more to do with the doughboys who assaulted me."

"Musa," the Advocate said. "I asked if you were okay. You said that you were okay!

"But, I think we have stalled long enough." Ninth Born placed Black Lazarus back into his robe and then rose his left hand. He intended to use his Dark Alchemy – Alchemy powered by the soul – to quickly recall his second Divine Aide, General Tariq ibn Ziyad, from the bottom levels of Heaven. But, as he did so, he was interrupted by Sara.

Now, Sara felt a nagging spirit growing inside her. Sara's frustration began to weigh so heavy on her being that she began to involuntarily float down to the jewel-encrusted floor, her feet touching the unevenness of the emeralds and gold carvings for the time. And as the Advocate turned toward the empty Throne of Judgment, Sara became even more frantic.

The Throne of Judgment remained open, for the AllGod had not been present in Heaven for some time and had rarely presided over the judgment of souls. In fact, the last time the AllGod had visited his kingdom was when the Rhythm & Blues singer the Blues King passed in the Earth year 2015. According to Heaven's Calendar, which is Color People Time (CPT) symmetrical, the great Blues legend's soul arrived in the kingdom 1,015 years ago. And the AllGod was there to give the Blues King a grand welcoming. Heaven was shut down for decades in celebration. It was a big spectacle.

The Ninth Born low key (secretively) found it dull to debate the merits of a soul with a chair in his father's absence. Still, it was the throne that the AllFather cast his wisdom of judgment within to render the ultimate verdict between Hell and Heaven. It was also the AllGod who established behind the Throne of Judgment the Chamber Kings in an arrangement of nine thrones made of bones to witness the greatness of Heaven's Judgment. And it was the Ninth Born the AllGod tasked to preside over this court as the defender of the soul until he is called back to Earth for the reestablishment of Paradise.

But Sara didn't know that shit. In her Redneck mind full of charming ignorance, anger, and fear, she thought that the absence of the AllGod, the presence of a frustrated Messenger, and the severe chatter of nine ol' ass kings was a sure sign that her judgment would be unfavorable. And, it is sad to say that, when most middle-aged White women have their backs pressed firmly against a wall, their inner Karen takes the wheel – rational thought be carlsontucking damned.

"Wait! Wait! Wait just one damn minute," Sara screamed as the Advocate, the God Sun, began to raise his left hand. "Was it the abortion?" Sara blurted out as quickly as she could, for she could not hold back her anxiety before the AllProphet. Then, in a SOHO Karen type of rage, she grabbed the Advocate by the right shoulder.

Sara attempted to turn the AllProphet around instead; she fell to the floor as flat as Becky's bottom. It became from that day forth, whenever a soul acted in extreme and erratic behavior before judgment, the court within the House of Sardis, including the nine kings and their court who sat behind the throne, referred to the action as the "Karen's Leap": the longest jump to the farthest self-serving conclusion.

"Uggghhh," Sara moaned as she ached from the spiritual pressure of the AllProphet's aura. "I was fucking sixteen – WTF! How the Alabama!" Sara continued as she lay prostrated, fingers pressed flat against the floor's engravings. She attempted to lift herself, but Sara could not move an inch, unable to bend the easiest joint. Then, the Advocate clapped his hands together, and the building shook. Sara didn't utter another word, for the AllProphet meant to interrupt her ass.

"W-T-F?" the Advocate questioned as he was beyond frustrated. "Woman, in Heaven we say WTT: what the tuck! Under Mormon Law, we use meaningless curses rather than utter actual ones that, when spoken by the spiritually powerful, would level the Kingdom of Heaven. But, this is my tucking house! So, silence yourself!" The Advocate possesses a voice that could hollow oak.

"I weigh the odds of your deeds, actions, and especially your mouth," the Advocate said as he sighed. He reached back into his Alan Guth for his pipe, Black Lazarus, discovering his lost goody bag full of the Purple Rhino Kush in the process. A bag the Advocate low-key received from Ishmael, a half-breed godling from the Redneck Riviera in which he called upon for the most exquisite load that was rare to come by in Heaven.

"Ah, Ishmael da plug. Thy strain is most potent for the occasion," the Advocate said as he sniffed the bag. He loaded a large pinch into his smoking pipe and mixed it with the remains of the God Bush. Ninth Born took a puff and exhaled the smoke, which entered the air as two circling doves the shade of lavender.

"Sara, Do you know why Ishmael calls this strain Purple Rhino Kush?" the Advocate asked Sara. "He calls it Rhino Kush, it acts one way which is smooth and easy but hits hard and cruel. Very deceptive."

In agonizing pain and terror, Sara sporadically responded:

"Ohhh God, no! I'm not deceptive. I am an honest Mitch. I don't know, Ishmael: not my plug. And I don't fool with the fish scale even if he was. I don't put pence in my nose and never tucked with opioids. And for the record: I don't care what Megan says. I don't do fraud by mail. I'm no tucking thief. I just boost a little, and I take from nobody but the corporations – they got it common. Alabama! I never even catfished a fella or let a man buy me dinner without giving him a little Stephen Mil (a sloppy blowjob focusing on the ugly bald head) in return. I'm fair. And why can't I curse? I love cursing. Let me up! I don't even know what's happening. Oh, God. I mean, Advocate. What's happening?"

The Advocate, with slight laughter, looked down at Sara, who was still prostrated, puffed, sighed, and said:

"No one without authority can curse in Heaven or in any

version of my father's presence. So here, most of us are forced by Mormon Law to use meaningless substitute curses in place of the ones that destroy our realm. It is not completely fun to substitute douchebag names for strong words full of meaning, but still enjoyable to say, to say the least." Then the Advocate looked off into the cloud-covered rafters of Sardis, which were brilliantly lit by a small sun that set closer to the distant ceiling that burned blue like a supergiant star.

"For your information, Sara: yes, abortions matter as all life matters." Then the Advocate thought about his days on Earth and how he never liked a Cotton-Gaetz, a hypocritical bitch, in uniform most likely purchased by the wealthy, the Pharisees in his First Life.

"Well, all lives except for a tucking constable. I send all but the souls of the purest Po-Po straight to the Confederacy! As Brother Bobby would say, that is my prerogative," the Advocate said. He had just noticed some of the Kingdom of Heaven's Mass Choir entering Sardis from its front entrance. They had been in the gardens just before Sardis that extend into the valley of clouds and colorful shrubbery just before Heaven's gates.

The Advocate then waved at Bobby Barisford, the RnB crooner who died in 2044 of congestive heart failure. As Bobby and Andre Wilks and other members of his select entourage of diva-like souls made their way threw the waves of the soon-to-be judged, they had a brief exchange of words.

Bobby, hoping that the Advocate would once again acknowledge him before the souls awaiting judgment, waved high into the air and yelled to Ninth Born, "High praise to the only one with 'God Sun' tatted on his belly! My brother, one king to another: stay in the faith, keep laughter and a smile on your face, and don't let them steal your peace."

"Are you reminding me of John 16:33, Brother Bobby? Or are you referring to a Psalm?" Ninth Born said as he lobbed the question across the House of Sardis in a humorous but open-minded inquiring tone. Bobby Barisford and his entourage continued walking toward the left side of Sardis, aiming at portal door E.1999.

"Neither, my Lord," Bobby said as he and Big Elle approached the door. "I was thinking more of Tupac Shakur and Bone Thugs, The Rose, Vol 2, track number two: Power of a Smile. You have great power in all things, especially in this situation, do you not, Sword Spitta? If you would be so kind as to light that God Bush back up again, you'll put a smile on many faces outside. We, who were with the rappers in the garden, took a whiff of your puffs and they were like the winds of April, like your father's breath of life. Even in the valleys beyond the gates, even in the woods with the African American and ROK Marines, their souls are high and as happy as tuck." Both Big Elle and the Advocate burst into laughter.

"Be kind and do not call me 'Sword Spitta' outside levels one and two, for the hard driven who labor in those places know me by that name. It is a name that provokes a different meaning there on those streets. You feel me?"

Then as one of the Sardis attending guards, a Theban Roman soldier under the command of the famous African Roman General, Maurice, opened the door for Brother Bobby. Big Elle looked back at the Advocate, patted his heart twice, and threw up the deuce (peace sign). In turn, the Advocate nodded and did the same.

The Advocate shook his head, having to swallow a chill lesson from such a rowdy soul. Ninth Born thought about the many strings he had to pull to get Bobby Barisford admitted into

Heaven. He pondered over Bobby's words as he took out Black Lazarus and cranked that pence, again.

"Ahh, Bobby," the Advocate said as he facepalmed himself, "A few billion more of those inspirational moments should be just enough penance to cover the first half of the 'Hump Around the World' Tour. Maybe." Then he returned to Sara, who was still pinned to the floor. The Advocate spoke.

"But by definition, I would not consider abortions murder proper as women have baseline authority over the mortal souls that enter or do not enter this world. This should be common sense, so much so I am sick of the argument. But, let's face it: after those Mitch-Gaetz Romans murdered me in the sickest and most outrageous way, even for those times, the world has pretty much screamed 'hold my beer' when it comes to murder. But, anyway. I digress.

"Although a soul is sent from many spiritual realms, Immortals, Prophets and our represented kingdoms agree that a soul must be installed inside the flesh at precisely the first heartbeat. The heartbeat is the start of life as it is viewed by us immortals and approved by all spiritual kingdoms, despite all other conflicts. This makes sense, does it not? I see the loopholes in the calamity of a soul's First Life, and thus, I champion the soul accordingly regarding all matters within my control.

"So, no, it matters not. A woman's responsibility for any choice forced upon her by a White man's rule takes a back seat to whoever wields false authority and whitewashes her control. A woman, who I hold up most as sacred, bears witness in the house of Sardis against her offenders and has the final say in these matters.

"But, on Earth, there are doctors, who have authority in medicine, and should be present to lead other medical professionals in consideration of the woman, the patient, and the merits of such a thing; this is the only counsel an Earth godling, a woman, needs in these matters. Where does this fall upon a soul that is twice trapped without a kind voice, neither one of emotional relief nor medical aid? And how would a person resist temptation in tough times of need if those that hold judgment over her do not consider her plea and trusted counsel? Is a woman tucked coming and going? A ding-a-ling doctor, a tucking nurse proper, a baby's father, a soon-to-be pauper, or even a king has no right to put a woman, in such a predicament! So, in the case of abortions, the Kingdom of Heaven has adjusted under Mormon Law and allows the young soul to return to sender. Right back to the Kingdom from which it came.

"Therefore, unless you consider the significant loss of each soul's fantastic potential, no harm, no foul. But for real, for real, if I am being fair, I can't tell you how many times a King Martin reincarnated soul has been returned to the kingdom, which is a sad affair considering that Martin is the only type of soul that Da Fam (ethic souls dear to the Advocate's heart) would genuinely follow. Why? I don't know, but he is truly a hard act to follow. Even I check myself when visiting him in the Thirty-Sixth Chamber.

"But, pence (shit)! It may have been the timing. When we last tried to reinsert Martin, it was the 1980s and the rich made abortions popular, like implants, botox, small phones, big phones, tiny phones and eventually smartphones. With most popular things, mortals consider their problems solved, no matter how trivial the creation or circumvention. Ehh, we are still working out how we place souls, so we don't fault you entirely for how souls are inputted into the body.

"The Kingdom of Heaven uses a Mormon-based system for

most things involving the soul's well-being keeping our eyes on the purpose of life and not its comfort. We don't account for epoch, race, sexual orientation, or culture when we stuff a soul in the flesh, its avatar, which is becoming a growing problem with the millenniums, so I am told. We may have to adjust, considering human medicine and science are not advancing fast enough to correct issues such as soul placement. Abortions, to be specific. For now, all the Mormon priests are like: 'A soul? What? Wrong body? Wrong parents? Wrong race? No such thing. Which is the right race? Who cares what body they get? It's all the same to Heaven.'

"In regards to abortions, even that misfortune is momentary as any aborted soul gets another opportunity at life at another time and human lineage. Some cultures call it reincarnation. But, a woman's soul is akin to God on Earth. Therefore, under the Laws of Judgment, we cannot hold offense over a godly soul when that soul does not have proper control over her being, which is her god-like possession.

"Thus, Heaven deems it not a choice and nullifies that commandment against you, a woman, the only portal into this universe and reality. Instead, it will be held against whatever royalty, politician, or governmental leader Heaven feels orchestrated a woman's hardship. Not that all Christian women get into Heaven, but at least nothing a man does to you in your First Life stands against you in your second. This is the power I wield as the Chief Adjudicator in Heaven. This is my recognition of the Earth godlings, which are womankind. It is fair and a proper adjustment, is it not?"

"I don't understand," Sara screamed from the floor. Nobody says anything like that. That's in no Bible I ever…" Sara began to say but cut herself short as she rarely read the Bible, which became very clear.

"Is that in there?" Sara asked, short of breath, moaning as she was firmly pinned to the floor, still frightened and confused.

"Is geometry in the Bible?" the Advocate said as he looked upon the millions of souls before him. "Yet, you guys found your way to the moon and back – Amazing! There's no Amazon-like way to prepare most mortal babes for anything other than walking in the shadow of my bronze feet, which involves a lot of crawling, rising, falling, and rising again. There are steps to this pence when it comes to salvation, just like geometry! For instance, you had ten commandments and four basic things to do: find food, find water, find shelter, and find your place in the Kingdom of Heaven through living a righteous life – basic-as-tuck! And yet, Bugattis exist like so much cardinal excess. And for what? Nothing about money or having abundant property is my way. Plus, speed limits are barely over a hundred.

"To be honest, I will admit that I have it on good authority that there is no better place on the planet Earth to drive and bust the tucking dashboard than Dubai – not that I can see it from here," the Advocate lamented. "But, is it wrong for the eternal kingdoms to expect spiritual advancement amid progress in science and medicine? Do you mean to tell me that we must lay the foundation as well as construct the roof? How much work from us immortals would mortals authorize? How much control would you give Heaven? How much would you condemn?" Sara became more frightened and was in dire need to rise, becoming a comfortability on the floor as is the thought process of Karen's when drawing near the end of their outbursts or rants. Although the Advocate spoke in concerning tones, his words fell upon Sara's ears like thunder. And for the first time in a long time since a Mega Karen's outburst or a Cracker heavenly revolution, fear and self-pity manifested in Heaven.

Now, Sara was at her wits' end as she lay prone, crying profusely. And like most Karens, Sara felt victimized by the order of Heaven and matters of life that she didn't understand. Then Sara heard some shit that really pissed her off and changed her whole crazy-ass demeanor. She heard snickering, a peal of low laughter echoing within the great Hall. But, the Advocate, who is a one-day, one-situation at a time sort of spirit, focused on his counseling of Sara.

"So, fear nothing in this house," the Advocate said. "Most heavenly truths are hard to hear and harder to bear, for they are not of White man's design. But, Sara, the die was cast long ago for woman and not against you, as the colonizers, of both the life and the spirit, would have you believe. That gray area of murder alone won't keep you out of Heaven since you are baptized and the ordained approver of life and not the likes of cowardly men who persist in making every aspect of the dreams of Heaven a nightmare."

The Advocate continued to stare off into the rafters as they appeared vibrantly lit due to the solar system surrounding the small blue sun beneath the distant ceiling. He puffed upon his pipe, Black Lazarus, sighed, and then said:

"You know," the Advocate stated. "If I'm being real, it is not your deeds and actions that vex me, for your sins are lightweight. It is time and agenda that I grapple with before the AllFather's throne," He took a long puff while turning back to the throne. And then the Advocate smacked the long-handled Black Lazarus on his right sleeve, emptying the pipe right before returning it into his robe.

"Be silent and maintain your peace for once, Sara. There is no place for fear in this great house! But, even here at the finish line, you compound my efforts with your words. Not only in life are we hung by the tongue, but in death also." And then the Advocate heard snickering coming from the distant side of his station, toward the left wall, and he did not care to hear that pence, no more than Sara.

Act Nine

The Unrighteousness of the Blessed

The janitors of Heaven were grouped together just outside the entranceway of one of the two hundred and twenty-two doorways set on the left wall of Sardis, laughing their asses off. The door, in particular, they stood within led to the promenade just outside the House of Sardis, within Heaven's gates, where they were as laborers assigned to attend. The Advocate, who grew more frustrated with the crawl and damned near stall of proceedings within his great judgment hall, had had as much as he could take for the moment.

"Enough!" the Advocate whispered, and the House of Sardis, an unmeasurable spacial construct, became silent. Now, most of the souls who served the House of Sardis and all the other holy houses that stand at the perimeter of Heaven – I believe there are twelve thousand altogether – are human souls who earned their place amongst the angels. But, most of these laborers are White men who entered Heaven on Mormon technicalities. They are men who, in life, erred on the side of caution in the face of temptation. They were neither severe in one way or another in the areas of divinity or wisdom, though collectively, they lived in many ages.

In their First Life, they were men who straddled the lines of sin and held a mind of indifference to the many vital matters concerning the soul: racism, sexism, politics, and culture. They are men who constantly prayed in their First Life but could only hear whispers of the Ether as most, who lived during eras of political fear, did not understand how to access the Ether through the proper herbs which is marijuana. Mostly, they are generals, truckers, doctors and well to do important men who now lead no mobs or armies. They are politicians who currently serve no continents, and church leaders, mostly Baptists, who never led souls to righteousness in the first place.

All that I have mentioned are those souls who in life were adjacent to the ordering or the carrying out of mayhem rather than having the audacity to do it themselves. And, although the Advocate hates nothing, these mortal souls are the false leaders the Dark Alchemist despises.

The Advocate is a clever and creative half-breed spirit and soul known by all of Heaven's courts as KACLI: King of All Clauses, Interpretations, and Adjudications. So, he amended Heaven's rules because he could not restrict a soul from Heaven that earned its return, however shady and technical the entry may be. So, he made it that all White men accepted into Heaven by technicality might only occupy the lower levels of the kingdom, levels one and two, where the grace of Heaven's power and pleasantries are the weakest. A location where the Whites could show gratitude and be thankful for their otherwise non-admission in the kingdom. And he made this so until the last of all earthly colonizers perish, nine generations, and balance of equality is established on Earth. Mortals should know that there are seven levels of Heaven, but only five in which the Advocate can grant access. And, for those meager White men, albeit only a few million or so in Heaven, he required them to labor for all eternity by working the maintenance crew of the first and second levels. And because his earthly ancestors are the children of enslaved people, he reminds all White men, every time he carlsontucking sees them, that the eternal service they perform is entirely for free.

These Crackers of varying waferage who manually labored in Heaven for free resented what they deemed an "open door immigration policy" regarding women, Blacks, gays, digitals, and non-Christians entering Heaven. And they especially resented servitude in a house such as Sardis, where they watched every soul they almost hated or seriously disliked walk willy-nilly through Heaven's Grand Door. These blessed souls felt cursed not to have risen to a higher heavenly abode.

But, as the Advocate has the final say in most things that transpire in Heaven, he saw fit to place them in Heaven in a way that matched their spiritual indifference in life. He decided to put their souls in the lowest parts of the highest Paradise. And these fuckers despise him greatly for it! They are the most envious souls in Heaven, only seconded by the spirit of the angels.

But, I suppose the janitors and caretakers of Heaven had been in Heaven a long time and had the opportunity to reminisce over past memories, melodies, and the slick attitudes of the enslaved people they encountered during their various times on Earth; all disastrous times described by the souls of women who walked in ebony skin.

Nevertheless, these lower caretakers would sing songs of lowkey disrespect to Heaven, its kings and their courts. By lowkey, I mean, that no soul who wanted to stay in Heaven dared openly voice a word of dissent, for the Ninth Born grew anxious and temperamental in awaiting his third life upon Earth and in that way, he was very much like his father. But of course, Crackers are Crackorish and will create chaos wherever they go, in life or in death.

Though in life they did not directly partake in savage deeds, they were idle and complicit when history called for righteous men to intervene. So, because of these Crackerish souls' envious disposition in Heaven, they resented and harshly commented whenever situations allowed for such behavior within the House of Sardis and at the gate of Addisu's Offspring.

One caretaker, in particular, Larry Kaminski, a former Air Force big-band director in the 1980s, was the main rabble-rouser who possessed heavy influence over the other caretakers who, like in life, were majority White men easily persuaded to act the victim. But, believe it or not, Larry was a soul that the Advocate was, for the most part, fond of simply because he had a soft spot for those who participate in acts he considered "good trouble." Ninth Born thought the boisterous dissenting soul was more humorous than harmful, and he had a fantastic range for the soul of a Jimjor Dane: an asshole who is completely lost. Nonetheless, Larry would sing his bondage songs and rub the Advocate wrong like any fucking clothing made from corduroy or like a 2008–2010 President Barrack Obama dealing with Vice President Joe Biden's first five hundred gaffs.

Larry was about in the Pavilion of E.1999, with other Crackerish caretakers, polishing the pavement, brick by golden brick, and cleaning the gold and stone columns lining the walkways, when the door labeled E.1999 swung open. Larry and the other Crackers, who were still petty bitches even in Heaven just as they were in life, watched the Advocate's temperament go from a righteous rage to a melancholy acceptance of the bickering soul of Sara. This angered Larry greatly. And so, Larry and the souls of the Cracker caretakers, along with the soul of one Black asshole who was so White in life that he manifested in Heaven in his police uniform, began to sing their "White Men are the

Martyrs" depressionary themed "ode."

Larry began with a four-bar intro into his unrest:

(Song: 'Don't You Care' – Beat BPM 118: https://youtu.be/7AJ_THgnJ8g)

(Larry)

"Ooh God, don't you care? Ooh God, do you even... care? Ooh God, please don't...

"Forsake us, don't you dare."

Every privileged asshole – dead or living – has that one culturally ignorant African friend who cosigns on all his pale-male apeshit. Why is that, you wonder? Well, it is simple. Just because a mortal is Black, doesn't mean that they know better, contrary to the believe that generational strife make all Black men wise. In fact, it is the opposite.

Many Black men are left wanting in life: wanting to belong, fit in or to be a part of the wining crowd. And so, as the soul of Officer Jeffery "Blue" Token heard Larry's soliloquy, he quickly picked up a mandolin that an angel left lying about the Pavilion and began to play it and sing along.

Token sang:

"...Ohh, Ohh, It's never fair. Ooh-Ooh, It's never even... fair.

"Ooh God – please don't forsake the pales. Ooh, God, don't you care?"

Sara watched as Larry, who appeared in Heaven in the best version of himself, a seventy-year-old limp dick sexist, danced his pear-shaped, balding manifestation around the Pavilion and sang. Larry deeply reminded Sara of the older man that got her pregnant those many years ago. And all of Heaven's Level One and Two White welfare souls, those of the most Crackerish nature and in Heaven on the slimmest of margins, joined in to annoy the Advocate, ridicule Sara's eventual entry into Heaven's higher levels, and to disturb the Advocate's Court.

"Ooh God, don't you care?

"We, the blue eyes and blonde-haired?

"Ooh God, please admit we're 'very special?' Ooh God, make it fair."

As the caretakers massed and began to cheer Larry on, he started to feel the "Caucasian Cocktail of Courage," concocted by the rowdiness of Heaven's most unsatisfied and privileged crowd. Larry began to swing his hips and dip with the rhythm of Token's mandolin. Then, Larry looked Sara in the eyes as she lay on the floor and sang:

"My daddy loved Christ.

"Loved the idea of a White Paradise. Devoted his whole life,

"To livin' right, every day, he prayed twice.

"And every single night,

"He would thank God for being just the right type of White, That Mmm-mmm, Sandra Bullock type of creamy white.

"Ooooh, that sounds nice.

"He hated nobody,

"He just loved being White,

"I ask: what's wrong with that?

"Why are White men soul's forever subjugated to the Lord's wrath?"

In a Redneck type of hoedown furry, the crowd of caretakers cheered and hollered more and more with each rhyme that Larry sang. Cheers, that did not praise the Advocate, but to embarrass one soul, Sara's. But Larry very firmly stood against women's ascension into higher planes, whether in Heaven or on Earth, he refused to give them proper praise. Token was feeling the tunes of his mandolin when several of Heaven's Karens, the only souls of females who are restricted to Level One, began to gather around him. Token once again felt his massive Black spirit rise amidst his soul, and at that moment, he renewed his thanks to Heaven for the souls of big bottom White women, and he smiled and prayed that he did nothing to upset them. He feared the tongue of the women of Heaven more so than he feared the very tempered and controlled Advocate. Larry continued on:

"This is making no sense. There's no forgiving this Mitch, Harassing our good Lord and Savior and pence?"

"Why is he so cool with it?"

"Why was my daddy not acquitted? – Hell Nah!"

"Bless your heart!" they shouted. "That ain't right!" they agreed.

"Let's start a war in Heaven." a few said in almost a whisper. But, at that moment, there wasn't enough of their mob to brew a properly motivating pot of Caucasian Cocktail, so they whispered.

"By the blood of Christ," some of the crazier Karens screamed. Mega Karens or Kellys are what they are called.

Now, the angels have often witnessed the souls of petty Whites attempt a coup just about every other dull moment in Heaven. So, this occasion seemed no different than the last or the time before that. And as the Angels lined the entirety of Heaven's perimeter at full arm-length apart, including the grand banisters of the E.1999 Pavilion, they looked on and shook their heads because the Crackers were at it again.

The Advocate, who was at the length of his wits and patience, could no longer bear the strain of split attention and stalling. In his best efforts to regain patience, order, and control of Sardis, he adjoined together the sigila Inscriptions – upon the tips of the middle finger and thumb of his right hand and uttered the words to the following Dark Alchemy cast:

"By the AllGod, I got nine beings inside of me, In unison, we are one of the multiple bodies, We, the Ninth Born to the AllGod, are immortality, I cast Dark Alchemy, Number 1,986 – UTFO:

"The Carpenter splits his personality: Come forth three Wooden Golems."

Although the ability to practice and thus master the Art of Dark Alchemy is an AllGod ordained discipline, only a handful of Dark Alchemists are accepted into Heaven, for the power corrupts most souls. Still, the Ninth Born is one of the strongest of those powerful souls allowed into Heaven's purview. His Dark Alchemy knows no bounds. for his soul, which is converted into energy required for the art, is a source of power that will never fade like the nine suns that represent him.

But, a mortal, especially a Christian, should know that the Advocate reserves his greatest significance for the mid-point of the Revelations. Until then, all malingering postponement of his triumphant return is his aggravation and greatest temptation, for in his heart, he just wants to wreck those and the descendants of those who violate his great name. When the Advocate returns to Earth, it will be with all his power and he will dawn his mighty helmet and armor as the crowned Warlord of Warlords. And, by the sword, will bring peace and happiness to the meek, but only after billions are purged.

But, this skirmish upon the House of Sardis and the gates of Heaven is not Revelations but a brief rehearsal his father has gifted his impatient son. One in which Ninth Born means to take full advantage. As long as he could keep Heaven's lowest born out of his way.

So, when the Advocate cast his Dark Alchemy within Sardis, the sigils inscribed upon his fingers sparked bright green flames.

Clouds of colorful gases rushed from the tips of his fingers. The gases were transmuted into water, dirt, and seeds that swirled about one another, composing three streams that moved like rivers. And as the streams gathered in the air and moved about like snakes, the Advocate commanded them into three places; the Pavilion of E.1999, the corridors beneath Addisu's Offspring, and the gardens just before Sardis.

Tremendous Alchemy it was! One stream of seeds and its package gushed into the Pavilion of E.1999 and struck the floor like a hundred hammers, penetrating the Pavilion's golden pavement. Then the embryos, water, and dirt penetrated, germinated, and grew roots that rumbled and rocked the foundation of Heaven, which takes enormous energy and spiritual pressure to even disturb.

At first, Larry and his band of selfish and self-centered upstarts were not worried, for they had no fear of the Advocate. After all, they had never seen him perform Dark Alchemy. Despite being in his presence for centuries, they solely based their understanding of the Advocate on Earth's Bible and his blood-soaked First Life.

Larry and the caretakers consistently failed to see and understand the Advocate, and true enough, all of creation in this universe. Most souls, even in Heaven, still viewed the Advocate as the earthling of 'goody-goodness' that oozed joy, patience, understanding, and orgasms wherever he went – pence posh! That's some Pelosipence in the old bullpen if I ever heard it.

In reality, the days the Advocate walked the Earth was a motherfucking blood bath by any immortal's standard! The Ninth Born lived for thirty-three tumultuous years, and from his birth to the last breath of his First Life, he had fucking haters. I mean, some real fully loaded tuckers, and I'm not Mansioning (bullshitting) you! From his first dawn until his last sunset, he was pursued by all demonic spirits and twisted souls. And as the Advocate lived the prototype righteous life, it ended spectacularly fucked up with him nailed high up on beams of wood with a nail in each hand the size of a Curtis.

(Curtis: A thick gold coin, the girth of an American fifty-cent piece, used as an official currency in the astral plane and made in KwaZulu, the Spiritual Paradise of the Zulu Nation. One side of the coin has the picture of the mortal Curtis Jackson, who was great and fearless in all lives, and the other is of AmanZulu, the prophet who knew no fear.)

(Mansioning: To mess with or exploit a person to insanity, literally death or mass shooting. To take someone for the shit-gulping fool that they undoubtedly are.)

Like anyone nailed to a cross and speared in the side, the Ninth Born immediately turned cold toward mortals, just as the AllFather did in the early days of man. I mean, this motherfucker felt played! Not only did the mortals he loved nail him to a cross, but nobody declared credit for the mayhem that ended the life of the ninth-born miracle of the AllGod. That's some sinister shit. Cold business, indeed.

However, what the world gained from the Advocate's slaughter was a well-documented matter and worth the effort in the AllGod's eyes. The AllFather thought that his ninth-born wonder, first-born to mortal flesh, handled himself exemplary. He would later brag and boast of his son's performance in the flesh and labeled all of his deeds some real rockstar shit. The AllGod was very pleased and proud – of himself, that is. See, the Advocate is the AllGod as a mortal being, and he lived the life that was intended, if ever the AllGod was human. So, the line of Eve provided the way, and so came the Ninth Born, the AllGod in the flesh. And the Advocate, who is the ninth miracle to AllGod, is his living testament for all to admire and cherish.

But, it has been long since the AllProphet accepted his post in Heaven and even longer since his resurrection. It has taken all of his patience to tolerate the antics of the Crackers this far, for Heaven was a post that he delayed, as you well know, for it was communicated in the Mormon Bible. But, as he has been in Heaven for quite some time, he has grown impatient and longs for battle. He was no longer a "turn the other cheek" type. He very much wished to fuck shit up!

Yes! The Advocate, the Warlord of Warlords, hungered for the Holy Purge that is the end of the Forever War and the last days of Revelations. It angered him and righteously so, for war is the last of his holy tasks. He has stewed for many eons, for there have been no spiritual wars in Heaven since Cain's soul was destroyed nor no spiritual battles on Earth since the last days of King Solomon. But Larry didn't know that shit! And that silly bastard reaped what he had grown with Ninth Born.

Behold! A massive Baobab tree quickly erupted from the mana that is the soil beneath the astral plane, and it began to grow and go through many seasons. The tree grew tall and wide with foliage and moaned and roared as it reverberated the gold pavement. The mighty Baobab tree, which radiated the AllGod's power, reached beyond the walls of the Pavilion. The gigantic tree swung and swooped around its powerful limbs, moaning from its transmutation. It grew anxious.

As the tree went through its seasons of growth, the Pavilion shook like a Lil John concert! Many angels were driven from appointed positions along its high walls, for the tree swung wildly. The centuries jumped, leaped, and flew from the tree with no genuine concern other than their comfort in duty and assumed established roles around the Pavilion just shy of the tree's wild and twisting swing. The ceiling of the Pavilion was like an invisible dome from the inside, but was solid construction to the view from the gardens of Addisu's Offspring.

    Initially caught up in their curiosity, as White souls often are, many in the E.1999 Pavilion reacted too late to avoid suffering brought on by the AllProphet. Souls closest to the tree could not escape its branches and were flung to the stone and gold pillars and jewel-encrusted walls that was the construction of the kingdom and stayed there while the tree was present. Some fell to the floor under tremendous spiritual pressure and were struck motionless. D'jon Hardgrove, who was still in the main body of Sardis and thus, not affected, ran to the door of the Pavilion just shy of the threshold and laughed and laughed and laughed some more at what had befallen the Crackers' Curiousity. Many looked to D'jon and watched as he hurried to the entrance of E.1999, laughing and saying the entire way, "Oh, pence! Oh pence! What have these Pale Souls done?" He was not in fear. And so, a vast swathe of souls followed D'jon as it seemed that he had familiarity with the Advocate and all that was transpiring.

Act Ten

A Texan Is What a Texan Does

Rupert Portman, who was not in shock at anything he had witnessed in Sardis, stood back amid the commotion caused by Sara and the Redneck caretakers of E.1999 and analyzed everything he saw, for he had planned to put it to good ol' boy use. And when the gaggle of souls followed D'jon to the entrance of the Pavilion, Rupert crept off to the vast hall of Sardis's until he reached its midsection.

Now, plenty of mortal souls lingered in the thick fog that covered the midsection of Sardis, and they greeted Rupert and welcomed Rupert as one of their own for his soul was pale and weak in nature as well. They were souls that stood and hovered with the damned, for they were bound for the Confederacy of Hell and many other awful places where the wayward of all Christianity dwelled. And because they were the discarded Souls of Sardis, left to linger, wonder, and wait, they all had an inkling of where they were going.

But, after hearing the Advocate himself make special concessions for women and the soul of a Latin child before that, it was as apparent to the wicked as it was to Rupert that their situation was dire. So, Rupert began to speak to the souls.

"Apparently, fellows…" Rupert said as he adjusted his ridiculously big belt buckle that still, even in Heaven, bent to the weight of his belly.

"There is no country for Cracker men, crumbling or alive," Rupert said to the souls he most thought would benefit his objective. But, almost as soon as Rupert started conversing, he was interrupted by the soul of a young soldier named Cody Madison. A little cocky motherfucker who, in life as well as death, often talked out of turn.

"Did you just see how he pinned that beautiful dame to the floor? It's a lovely floor, and I would like to pin her down too if you know what I mean, but come on!" the young mortal in the allure of an Army uniform said to Rupert. Rupert laughed as he very much enjoyed the humiliation of women.

"Lol, that's a good one. You are a smart young soul," Rupert interjected. "What's your name, soldier?"

"It's Cody Madison, sir," Cody said as he smiled and stood tall.

Rupert immediately picked up on Cody's vibes and knew instantly that the kid died a virgin, never knowing the sweet nectar of a woman. Rupert used that knowledge to his advantage.

"Are you all right, Son?" Rupert asked. "I'm sorry you had to see that awful display.

"You didn't like what went down upfront, now did you?" Rupert hoped to exploit the Corporal's nature by keeping him chatting. But, it didn't take much coaxing for Cody to get lost in thought and what he thought he saw. The passions of the damned are always and foremost on the cursed minds and hearts. And as Rupert had hoped, Cody continued to spew shit from his thin pasty mouth.

"Alabama! No, mister, not at all! Did you see the yams on that chassis?" Cody asked. "And those cans? Geez!" As he described Sara, who was either a woman or a Buick in his mind, Cody turned to his fellow soldiers for approval – a little dose of the cocktail, I suppose. And, like clockwork, all those sheep-minded motherfuckers in Cody's Division nodded and agreed. All except for a few hundred African soldiers who, as a fraternal brotherhood within the Army, learned to be wary whenever White people gathered in large groups. Cody, who was a doughboy in the First Great War of Earth, rambled on:

"You just don't treat a swell girl like that where I'm from, if you know what I mean? Those chappies down in Brownsville, maybe you can smack them around like that, but never a vanilla wafer like Susie-Q – Whew! I tell yah: she's the type of broad you wanna trap in the kitchen and over the years watch all her dreams vaporize like the steam from a good old pot of boiled meat."

"Ha! Ha! Ha!" the mud and blood-covered young men voiced their laughter as they jeered in favor of the boisterous young soul, their earthly hero, and the senior officer's favorite Non-Commission Officer. In life, the young lad must have reminded them of their sons, grandsons, neighbors sons, uncles, brothers, etc. But it is clear that even in death, their bias creates an allure everywhere the White soul goes, but I digress. The young soldier rambled on:

"I mean, I wasn't that close to the front, and still, that Gaetz was a nice fit! That was no regular White girl's pancake Gaetz, no sir. That was a bloomer-zoomer-baby-boomer if I ever saw one!" Cody said. Then Cody became noticeably upset over the Advocate's treatment of Sara. Cody and all twenty thousand or so soldiers leaned into Rupert as Cody noted the following:

"But the big guy attacks the dames!" Cody said as his Division moaned their disapproval with random sounds harmonizing like a barbershop quartet. "And only the White women like a thug in a back alley. Karens he calls them like that's some excuse, ignoring the very thing that makes them special and privileged. But I swear if you are the soul of a fifty-year-old female Christian African, then step right up and roll out the red carpet! It's a tickertape parade and this is freakin' Holy Harlem. He doesn't seem like the White, Industry Supply-side Jesus that I learned about in Sunday school, if you get my drift." Then, as Cody leaned back and folded his arms, so did the Division. All except the two hundred who did nothing that the White boys did out of caution. Cody continued.

"But, as I said," the young Corporal continued, "I wasn't that close. Maybe he ain't no Gaza Gangster," the soldier said. Then Cody articulated that a Gaza Gangster was a Gaetz (ass) of a person, or people, who would covet another person's spouse, property, wealth, or land. It was a term taught to Cody by the soul of a Syrian Private named Louis Fatima, who was far behind Cody and the Division, grinning like Flava Flav in a room full of tall European women.

Now, Louis had convinced Cody moments before they died that the entirety of the ancient world, or as Louis clarified, "the United Nations of the World," regularly used the term Gaza Gangster to describe a colonizing crook. Private Fatima grinned widely and nodded at Rupert as Cody explained, for Louis knew who the Texan was and why the Texan was at the gates of Heaven. And Louis continued to watch, sniggling hard, as Cody talked his tucking Gaetz off, distracting Rupert for some time. Cody continued:

"And another thing, unless my eyes are taking me for a ride, it sure looked to me that the AllSavior was a freakin' Jew and not like the pictures from Sunday school either, if you get me?" Cody said. "I was expecting the red-haired and bearded Viking that I grew up with. This guy looks like a freakin' Jew who shouldn't even be in this house of the gentiles." Then, Private Louis interjected:

"Oh, he's a Jew, all right," Louis said as he stared intensely at the Advocate, who was smoking God Bush out of Black Lazarus at the time and deliberately not sharing any with anyone else nor asking.

"He could swallow a penny and pence a Curtis or two he's so much a Jew."

Louis looked down at the jewel floor and then all over the immaculate room and said: "Smokin' Alabama (a burning Hell)!" as low as a whisper would allow.

"As far as I know about Jews, all the gold trimmings in Sardis could have been minted directly from the Advocate's *mukhara* (Arabic for ass); he's so much of a Jew." The Army division laughed and then sang a Barbershop-style melody of Lord T.I.P.'s hip-hop song they believed to be about the Advocate on modern-day Earth:

"Mmmmhhhmm, Jews!

"From land to land, they ain't nothing but a troublesome band, Always in a situation, man, always on the hustle, fam. Forever, in our minds, they live life in a bubble, damn, Jews, Jews, Jews! Jews are a blessed hustler's clan."

Louis grinned harder.

"Awe, Alabama," Cody reiterated and smiled. Then, turning to Rupert, Cody said with a severe tone:

"You were there, mister. I could see you from the rear. You were behind the uppity Negro – not that I see Coloreds. What happened to the dame, sir?" the young Corporal's soul asked.

"Young man, what tucking year did you die?" Rupert asked Cody, astonished by Cody's choice of words. He paid particular attention to Cody's muddy, torn appearance. He was reminded of a grandfather he had never seen other than the pictures that set upon his grandmother's chest of drawers.

"Geez, mister. We've all talked about it, the boys and I, and none know exactly when we died. But we've been waiting here in the heavenly Apple for a few decades now. Well, at least in Sardis, I guess. There were other soldiers here, but they went through Heaven's Grand Door long ago." Then Cody stared at Rupert and thought for a moment, chipped some of the caked mud from his uniform, and pulled a notebook from his cargo pant pocket. "Alabama (Hell), mister! I can't even tell you what year it is on Earth." Cody looked down to review the scribblings on his waterproof notepad.

"I just have these coordinates, you see, here on my *lil darling* for where the boys and I, my Division, were waiting to attack the Hindenburg Line. It was over the hill of this farm, but we never saw beyond it." Cody stared at the jeweled floor of Sardis as if he had lost his thought. Rupert licked his lips and became engorged, for nothing turns a White man on more than a younger White male that he could mold. After a moment, Cody spoke again.

"All I know is that that tucking *Tommy Cotton* (dick bag) said we had to do it, so we did! The boys and I call the first lieutenants back on the base '*Tommy Cottons*' because the doggone doggy's uniforms never got dirty. And their dicks are small, like cotton balls. We call them Tommy Cottons."

"By Demitri!" Rupert said as his cotton ball throbbed harder.

"God bless you boys," Rupert said, just shy of stroking his White pride. He took a step back and looked upon the twenty thousand infantry and tank troops surrounding Cody, packed tightly amongst each other. More mortal soldiers died with Cody and his Division of the young and poor that day, but not all souls ascend to Sardis, only the Christians.

You should know that Heaven uses many holy algorithms that monitor a soul's every step. The Kingdom follows a strict version of Mormon Law and believes that what sins a soul repeats in one life would be repeated in the next, and should not weigh the Advocate down with unnecessary bureaucracy. And so many souls are judged by Heaven's algorithms before their earthly end. Some Christian souls go directly to Hell or Purgatory, for they have proven themselves untrustworthy in all forms of life.

Some mortals would question whether that's fair or not. I ask, why the fuck do you care if you never plan on living righteously in the first place? See! And the perpetual sinner clogs the books of Heaven up no more. Moving on...

Rupert nodded, lingered a long-lasting and jittery thumbs-up as he viewed the Division, and winked his right eye as Whites often do when they are about their mischief. But Rupert lost a few of the soldiers as soon as his corny ass began to speak.

"And only a few Coloreds amongst you!" Rupert said. "That's excellent."

It was September 29, 1918, and upon that day, every American cavalry and tank Division that came to the battlefield west of Villers-Hélon in support of the Allied forces was, unfortunately, an inexperienced soldier up and to the exact moment of death beneath the Saint Amand Farm that set upon that hill. *Two hundred or so African American troops* were allowed to serve in that Army division, which was an incredible honor for them to die with their countrymen in the eyes of Heaven. Sacrifice is a big fucking deal, after all.

But, when Rupert spoke his well-meaning disrespect, the African soldiers gritted their teeth, sighed underneath their breath, and showed no emotions at all. They had been trapped there in Sardis with their Division knowing no peace or safe passage to the Advocate. Cody and the Division of the Damned had prevented the African two hundred progression farther into Sardis, for Cody and his bunch knew their day would come and would not see their brothers ascend further than themselves. So, the African two hundred, the descendants of enslaved Christians, therefore, Christians themselves, stayed in Sardis and were implored by the cursed Crackers to remain. And the longer the African two hundred remained in Sardis, the more their expectations for Heaven resembled those on Earth.

Rupert found the African purview to be acceptable Blacks, for they said nothing, which meant that they were complicit in his eyes, and he liked that a lot. But, Rupert did not know the inner workings of Heaven or the Advocate, who is the King of Loopholes. He did not think that the Africans were bound for Heaven's upper levels based on the merits of slavery. Although Heaven was his enemy, Rupert only could see that his enemy was like him, for it is his culture to hate and love at the same time. So he ignored the African two hundred and spoke on as if he did not see color or, in this case, the ebony allure of an African soul.

"You are some Real Americans (you are White people)," Rupert said, "and precisely the sort that I was hoping to find here." Rupert scanned the crowd of servicemen, hoping to see a glimmer of privilege and evil in their eyes. Yet, he found none, just the poor misfortune of inexperienced leadership and slow-reacting government.

"I am in Sardis on purpose," Rupert said, "and, according to Mormon Law, they cannot keep me out. I have used an Ol' Mitch-Gaetz Magic, the lost magic of my folk, to be here in Heaven at this precise moment."

Sardis thundered in reaction to curse words spoken within it. The floor began to shift and open beneath many of the soldiers' feet, devouring them whole in brimstone flames. The other Corporals of the Division crouched down and became frightened and, thus, grew weary of the Texan's talk of mutiny. Cody stared at the Texan for a moment, stood up, and said:

"Pale Face Phuckery? The forgotten magic of the Cracker Nation? Pelosi's (stampeding bulls)!" Cody said. "That's a wise old tale that my great-grandmother from Dixieland used to tell us kids. It was a bunch of Pelosipence, something about the golden age of White trickery, which was directly after the Civil War and some here say when somethin' call 'opioids' were introduced. But in my great-grams day, she said they let the Blacks live in their houses for a bit and pretended to give them land. Told them that they were citizens." Eighteen thousand or so soldiers that still remained stood proudly as they dusted the caked mud and blood from their uniforms and laughed. Then Cody said:

"You know, it took me years to hear the story because we could never get through it without laughing ourselves silly!" Cody said as he laughed, holding the part of the soul where the stomach would be.

"Anyway, she told me you would need to shed a lot of blood to power magic like that, so a blood bath it was. Sir, listen, I don't know if you are paying attention, but you are stuck here just like the rest of us. You are here until your number is called, and when it's called, you'll be like my buddies, the newly and dearly departed, wishing that you were back in here where the flames didn't reach. Then Cody looked around at his pasty lads and said:

"As you can see, there's nothing you can do about it." The Texan grew angry.

"Now, wait just a cotton pickin' minute!" Rupert said. "You boys should know that I have sacrificed my First Life at the behest of the Gnome King, Jeff 'the Javy' Jefferson," and the

Golden Idol President, the Great Magada Gaga, the Covfefe, former President Grifford 'Grift' Griffington, III. Yes! The Orange Bandit himself. We, who descend from the Children of Cain, and those of the Neanderthal bloodlines, will be cursed no further, and therefore I come to petition Heaven on account of all White men – dead and alive – who crave the constructs of privilege and hypocrisy. And we will petition Heaven with the sin that the Kingdom lusts for, but do not boast: war."

Cody straightened up and offered no more offense. He was familiar with the Gnome King, an immortal who resides high above the Hell mount known as Alabama, which is considered the physical State of Hell located on Earth. Cody also knew that the tiny angry gnome tolerated no form of disrespect unless it was from the Covfefe himself, who was royalty in the Confederacy of Hell.

"Sir, I didn't mean to be belligerent," Cody said with deep humility and lust. He knew that any adventure involving President Griffington, who was phuckery foretold, would prove an outrageous, dangerous, and unruly affair.

"What would you like us to do, Captain? You are in charge!" Cody said eagerly as the whole troop leaned in over his shoulders. Then Rupert smiled.

"Boys," Rupert said while unbuttoning his plaid shirt, revealing a large pentagram tattooed on his stomach. It was a pentagram of the seven wounded elephants of the Republican Party, all engulfed in brimstone and blood, having many broken tusks. And though Rupert's bitch ass was not a Dark Alchemist like the Advocate or the Advocate's aids, the Texan found a way to activate a magic spell within Sardis, using the spiritual power that is always abundant at the gate of Abraham and his offspring.

"In the next few moments," Rupert said as he flailed his shirt apart and tucked it behind his voluptuous love handles that resembled split baby cheeks. "The Children of Cain and those of the Descendants of the Neanderthals shall engage Heaven on multiple fronts. And you are an essential part of what we do here for America. Now, we shall break many ancient seals to show Heaven that we, the Republicans, have not forgotten the first days and old ways, and the first oaths before the coming of the godling Jew, and certainly before he left the Knights of Riviera and the Counsel of Nabu unchecked – and he, the AllGod, dares keep Odin, the true 'All-Father,' hidden from us while those heathens run free and wild? We think not! We seek the days of Odin and we shall have them! We too seek the hard days of Revelations and we shall have that also. And we shall not allow the finality of the Forever War be dictated by the flesh of a false American such as Carnegie Black, the Wrath Writer, the so-called Carnivorous Alchemist, or any decline of Ramses III powerless seed. All realms belong to Real Americans (White men) or, at least, the corporations that are as pale to the core as we are to our hearts."

Many soldiers of the Caucasian persuasion sipped the cocktail of Caucasian courage that Rupert had just stirred before their souls. They became aroused at the prospect of one last war. And with sorrow in their hearts and the rage they built up as the underprivileged of Sardis, the Texans Division of the Damned was formed, and they marveled at the idea of serving the war godling, Odin.

Act Eleven

The Rising Dead below Heaven

But, Louis Fatima, a Wrath Breaker, a Dark Alchemist who destroys kingdoms – physical and spiritual – from within, was hip to all Rupert had come to Sardis to do. And one by one, Private Fatima pulled the African soldiers into the fog of Sardis, hiding them from the Division.

"Be quiet, all of you," Louis said. "Though we are in the mouth of Heaven, the enemy is all around, and it is their teeth that grip us now, even the Advocate, for he and everyone else is cut off from the Ether at this moment and may not be fully aware of the pending attack." And then, the Sergeant of the African two hundred, Elijah Jemima, whose descendants were robbed of their molasses and corn processing plantation after his demise, replied to Louis.

"Pence, pence, and pence again!" Sergeant Jemima said. "Will I ever be rid of war and all this Redneck buffoonery? The White folks act a Gaetz wherever they go, even the astral plane. My grandmother was terrified of each and every one of those carlsontuckers like the ones of her time were the boogy man or something. I am tired of all this pence and what I want now is peace, not more pence. I died at the age of twenty-four and could not be happier about it, although I do leave loved ones behind. Great woe! How I crave for peace. Not even here in Sardis after all this time have I found even a glimmer of it. Alas! Heaven is just like Earth: a confrontational mess absent of rhyme or reason. I would choose Hell to be rid of these Crackers if I did not already know that Hell is known in all the secret places as the Confederacy. And all of its Satans are carlsontucking bigoted as pence. Tuck my Second Life!"

As Jemima spoke, Louis led the two hundred African soldiers through the fog and to a secret door that laid upon the floor about the rear-midsection of Sardis and sent them down its steps, one by one. Louis, who treated his Dark Alchemy as a cruel joke and made it a point to take nothing seriously, even death to a certain extent, laughed at Elijah and shook his head.

"Will you second-guess the entirety of your Second Life, Sergeant Jemima, just as you did the first?" Louis said to Elijah. "This is what I know of you, my friend, though my second time on Earth was short-lived. I cannot maintain a body in the physical world and was just there long enough to fall with you before that farm which was my second time falling before some random hill. But, I am Babylonian, and just like you, many of us died as holy warriors, never mind the cause.

"I died fighting against the Tribes of Israel, whose very horde rolled over all the lands south of the Mediterranean as if it was a mighty wave from that sea. I, too, was twenty-four when I died. I fell at the gates of Babylon the first time it was destroyed. So, yes, you are right to lament, for your first death is still fresh upon the spiritual mind." Anger grew on the face of the young sergeant, whose rank signified the number of fallen predecessors and not years of service.

"My friend," Louis said, "every soul that becomes a spiritual warrior knows even at a precious age that the supernatural world is more violent than the physical. We know fear before anything else in this world. So, in all circumstances, we must cherish the

First Life.

"But now, you must accept that spiritual warriors have little choice in any life that may be lived or death the universe might give. We whose souls are touched by the AllGod's Mark of Abel, and thus, grow a Dark Core to power the spiritual science of the universe, know to trust in all that the ALFAMAK (Father of All Mankind) has ruled, regardless of understanding. As they say: 'in for a penny, in for a pound.' Things are as the AllGod wanted. However, it is solely up to you whether you stand or quiver, a coward or righteous deliverer. Anyway," continued Louis, staring into Elijah's eyes, "there are not many Dark Alchemists allowed within Heaven's walls. This is most likely why the Advocate, who was young when he first ignited his Dark Core, left you to the will of your division. What use would you be in Heaven if you would not use the power granted to you in the face of the unworthy? How would you be of service in the AllGod's Kingdom? Have you ever wondered why the Advocate is out here on the skirts and not within toasting champagne and toppling the virgins?"

"Who gets excited over virgins?" Elijah asked as he stared back at the fog. "My cousin was the first of us to activate his Dark Core, and my grandmother, Sukey, couldn't be happier. She was a Dark Alchemist herself, so no one was more pleased, for her Alchemy was extraordinary, and she wanted nothing more than to teach it to her African descendants. She taught Scipio, my cousin, his first cast, which was a cast to shift rock beneath the Earth. He mastered it, and together they rotated the Earth to convert underground springs to our wells from miles away.

"But, as you know, few alchemists die a natural death. The draining of the soul takes a hefty toll. Converting the springs was too much for her worn Dark Core to handle. It cracked, severing her Alchemy from its energy source and nullifying her contracts with nature, leaving her defenseless.

"Alas! The Children of Cain were watching. And so, a demon of the Confederacy, a half-breed, came for her one summer's solstice. The demon was fierce, and her Dark Alchemy was incredible despite having a malignant soul! She murdered my Scipio and grandmother Sukey, and the Confederate assassin did it with great lust that burned like fire in her eyes, even though her expression was cold. I was only seven when this occurred, and pure fear caused me to activate my Dark Core. So, I am cursed repeatedly, for the demon let me live so that I would be someday worthy of her skill, or so she said." Elijah watched as his comrades disappeared down the dark and steep corridor beneath the floor. Then Louis spoke again.

"I tell you, Elijah," Louis said as Elijah approached the entrance. "Now that you are a Traveler – a powerful soul forever separated from flesh – you may be one day worthy of the ALFAMAK's attention. But, just as your grandmother Sukey and your cousin paid a price, you must decide how you will satisfy the AllFather in the Forever War, for it is a journey one should plan well. But, know, whatever you choose, the curse of oblivion lies ahead for most of us Dark Alchemist – this is the cruelty of it all. So, my friend, will you use your power for the ALFAMAK or against him? After all, you ignited your Dark Core and converted the soul's energy of light into the dark. You announced yourself to the universe before the end of your First Life, which means you are fair game in your second one."

After listening to the Wrath Breaker, Elijah bit his lip and took a deep breath, realizing his frustration would be fruitless. He stood at the entrance of the tunnel way as most of the African two hundred made their way deeper within the stepped tunnel.

But then, Louis stopped him upon the first step, grabbed him by the allure of his arm, and said:

"Heaven may not be for you, my friend," Louis said, "although I am sure you lived a righteous life. But, I'll take you and your comrades to a position where the Advocate will need us the most, and then you can decide how you will live your Second Life.

"However, you should know that the Council of Nabu is not blind to what has been planned here, nor are we ignorant of the ruse, which was the sacrifice of the Texan's soul. Separatists of the Confederacy have made alliances with the Children of Cain and the Neanderthal's Brood. They plan to attack Heaven on several fronts, and worst, they plan to awaken Odin.

"The January 6, 2021 attack on the U.S. Capitol, all those years ago, was a necessary event, for White Phuckery is magic that depends on fear and deception. The ritual the Rednecks and the Neanderthals performed together on that hollow ground broke a heavenly seal, the Seal of Benjamin Banneker, which allowed the sacrificed to appear in Sardis for judgment at their choosing.

"And it is the year 2030 on Earth, the correlating year they have chosen to show themselves in Heaven. But, we, the Black Knights of the Riviera, have a plan!"

When Louis and Elijah reached the bottom of the steps, they stumbled into the backs of the soldiers who halted just beyond the stairway inside the massive corridor junction.

"What is this? Why have you stopped?" Louis asked the soldiers.

A PV2 (Private Second Class) from the African troop responded, "You, you come move these motherfuckers aside cause I'm not fucking touching them!" Suddenly the PV2 realized that he could curse and became more fascinated with his long-lost ability than the nightmarish scene before him. So, he danced about the troop and the undead, cursing up a storm. And laughter was all about the corridor because everyone loves a fool.

"Ha! Yes, a mortal soul can curse down here as we are not exactly within the borders of Heaven," Louis said as he took a lamp from one of the soldiers and walked into the darkness before them.

"Before Harriet Tubman took her post upon her chariot that seeks Heaven's lost souls," Fatima said as he shoved his way past the bracing and rattled soldiers. "She convinced the Mormon High Counsel of Heaven to prep the Kingdom should there ever be another war. And, because they admired her and hung on her every word, they agreed," the Babylonian said as he moved through the junction, still laughing at the PV2.

Louis laughed as light from the lamp bounced about the corridor as if its glow was a pendulum's bob. But, as the light danced about the underground space that, though damp, dazzled in the glow, the African two hundred stood frightened upon seeing glimpses of the undead soldiers before them. They stood the average heights of men, covered in Arabic and African garb, shoulder to shoulder, standing amid the wide corridor junction. The skin of their flesh smoked, and it burned as fast as it regenerated upon their bodies.

Louis continued to laugh as he reached the top of a short platform in the center of the intersection, where he stood above the shrouded figures. As he stood above them, scanning the underground corridor with a great grin on his face, he reached into the chest of his soul and pulled out his Book of Life. Then, the Wrath Breaker threw the book into the air before him and uttered these words:

"By the Mark of Abel, the AllGod holds Solomon's oaths fulfilled,

"I, Louis Fatima, Wrath Breaker of Nabu, breaks the soul's First Seal, Forth comes thy book, converted, and bound to the fourteenth Earth, Wipe clean thy First Life, reveal great works of an immortal's birth."

When Louis spoke those powerful words and kicked that rhyme with steady nerve, the universe answered his call. The constructs granted Fatima permission to control his Book of Life and convert it with the soul's energy so that it may serve as the Wrath Breaker's Book of Alchemy and anchor his wayward soul to the Tower of Nabu. It was 539 BCE (Before Caucasians Existed) when Fatima fell at the gates of Babylon, and his soul was trapped in the physical realm by the Mark of Abel. The Council of Nabu rescued the Dark Alchemist from oblivion and set him on a most righteous path.

So, his allegiance is to Nabu, who he will serve until the end of the Forever War, the end of days for all wicked souls and the fallen things. And because Nabu has claimed his soul, Louis can manifest his Book of Alchemy and use its prescribed casts – alchemic rhymes – to regenerate the flesh that once was, but not without cost.

Louis gritted his teeth short of screaming as flesh began to form around his soul.

First, his bones grew where his soul stood, agonizingly fulfilling the structure of a human's bones. Then muscles and organs developed as veins rose from his newly formed feet, barely meat, just cartilage, and toes. The veins shot upwards, spreading all around and within his soul. Lastly, his skull grew, and the vibrant purple glow of the Dark Core amidst the center of his soul became hidden behind organs and gore, and his soul could be seen no more.

Louis fell to one knee, still holding the lamp in his right hand. After regaining his energy, he rose, cast Dark Alchemy over the light, and began to speak as he dropped the lamp into a transmutation circle of the star of David. When the transmutation circle reappeared, it did so high above their heads. And out of the spiraling ring of energy that is a transmutation circle dropped the light, absent receptacle and high above their heads.

"American soldiers," Fatima said, facing Elijah and his troop from atop the platform. "I would like to introduce to you, General Hamilcar Barca And these lovely fellows that stand before you are the Horde of Carthage, 247th."

When Elijah whipped his soul completely around to view all of what he considered monstrosities, he went apeshit! He walked forward, astounded by the walking undead as the rest of his troop nearly befouled the room with their bowels. One soldier fell to the floor in horror. The Sergeant watched the General as portions of Hamilcar's face burned and disintegrated in the air and became enraged.

"They are demons, Fatima! They are the undead and absent of the AllGod's light!

"Are you a necromancer or a righteous Dark Alchemist?" Elijah asked Louis, scolding him for what he found unholy. But, before the Wrath Breaker could answer, the young Sergeant ran toward the General, knocking back some of the undead soldiers in his path, and said:

"Are you the general of all these troops? Do you lead these dead men here?" Elijah asked the Carthaginian statesman. Bewildered, General Barca looked at the Wrath Breaker for direction. But, after receiving no reaction from the General, Elijah ran toward a giant, muscular troll as it slobbered profusely next to Barca.

"What sort of alchemic beast is this troll?" Elijah said, looking the ravenous, rage-filled changeling up and down.

"I know for certain," Elijah said, peering at the beast, "this troll is a changeling, a Child of Cain, spawned by the first of the Satans, the Archangel Samuel, who swore to wipe out and enslave all those who carry the Jemima name. This thing is of great evil and must be silenced."

"I wish that I had more time to explain, but haste won't allow it, for the war is coming soon," Louis said as he stood behind his Book of Dark Alchemy, its pages flipping unprovoked as it hovered just before his waste.

"No," Louis replied, "the General does not serve me but serves the Carnivorous Alchemist, the Wrath Writer. Yes, these soldiers are under Barca's command. However, they all are bound to the Jurican's Bow, which is the flying ship of the Wrath Writer. They have spoken the Oaths of Solomon and will serve the Jurican forever, or until Carnegie the Black releases him."

"Never mind the damn dinosaurs, carnivores, traveling carnies, or whatever that shit is!" the Sergeant angrily replied. Then, Elijah ran back toward the Horde of Carthage, whose flesh continued to burn away. They all stood beneath the protectorate of Heaven, where spiritual shields weaken the wicked. With great intent, the Sergeant pointed into one Carthaginian's face, then all the undead, and said:

"Well, check this shit out! He's a demon, that things a demon, and since the rest are dead men with no souls, all these fuckers are demons! What the fuck?" Then Elijah stomped over to the troll again and said:

"And look at this thing! This monstrosity! It is, without doubt, the most frightening, repulsive, evil and chaotic beast I've ever seen. It reeks of deceit and lies. There is no way that thing will serve the righteous." The African two hundred nodded or shook their heads depending on what Elijah said.

"Sergeant," Louis said, still recovering from his transformation, eyes still focused on his book. "Although you are more familiar with the supernatural than your troop, there is still much you do not know," the Wrath Breaker explained.

"No!" Fatima said, growing weary of Elijah's rant. "They are indeed demonic souls; however, not demons for they have never seen the palaces of the Confederacy. They are bound by the Oaths of Solomon and cannot act at whim," Louis said as he flipped through his Book of Alchemy, preparing for the assault. "But fear not the troll for she is bound to me and must do my bidding regardless of want."

Then the giant, rippling troll, who hunched her back over to avoid the junction's ceiling, wiped the drool from her mouth and smiled. And with a Georgian accent, she looked into Elijah's eyes and said:

"This war must be invested, and every soul, wise or wicked, must be held to full accountability – all say he the AllGod, Amen. And, all who swore the Oath of Solomon must uphold the Mormon Laws and PROTECT our Heaven's border. Yes, the Children of Cain and the Neanderthals are both my cursed brethren. But, if they are ENABLING and ALLOWING this ongoing invasion into the Heaven and attacking the agents of Heaven and the Jew who commands many space lasers, then it is breaking the AllGod's laws, thus breaking their oath. Don't worry, young Sergeant, I love eating the souls of troops. This is true, but ye' shall have no need to fear me, the M.T.G."

Elijah was blown back by the twisted spiritual pressure of the beast, but most of all, its foul breath and high-pitched voice.

Her voice echoed through the chamber though she whispered. Her words fell upon their ears like a spell, for they were forgotten as soon as they were spoken.

"The M.T.G.?" Elijah reluctantly asked.

"I am better known in the depths of the Confederacy as the Habitual Liar's Shield Maiden, the Magada's Troll Guardian, but you may call me Large Marge, the Green Troll," the troll said proudly, for she loved the lies she told on Magada Gaga's behalf. But it was the Black Knights who captured the wild troll. A beast like no other who was oily and sweated profusely.

"How did you come to control such a beast?" Elijah asked Fatima while still staring at the troll, whose blonde hair curled and dripped from the weight of her bodily fluids.

"I'm glad that you bring that up," Fatima said, staring at the two hundred unclaimed African souls that stood in the junction. "Elijah, have you ever heard of a philosopher's stone?"

Act Twelve

The Texan Lays an Egg

"Lean in, boys," the Texan said. "Come in tighter and hug one another, feel each other's goodness." By "goodness," Rupert meant "Whiteness."

"Cody, son," Rupert said, staring into the Corporal's eyes, "go ahead and put your hands on my belly and press the picture firmly." Cody was reluctant to touch the jiggling allure of the politician, but, like the souls of most White boys, he did as he was told.

"Go on now, boys, and get in there, get in there good," the Texan said, leaning back and feeling the soldier's energy as it charged the pentagram on his fat. Cody's hands sunk deeper into the inscription on the Texan's belly. And with the power of the soldiers' souls firmly connected, Rupert spoke his incantation to his bitch-like magic, the souls were ripped from the control of Sardis, and all eighteen thousand or so souls were sucked into the Texan's belly, with room to spare. Then he spoke to the Constructs of the One Reality and begged them to hear his plea.

"Oh, ancient constructs, ye' influential performers and programmers of the automated, repetitive, and pre-defined universe, hear my cry. I, Rupert Emilio Portman, a descendant of the Children of Cain, a true Republican, call upon you with the blessing of the all-knowing Mother Earth in all her mighty names. Que, Qaia, the Q'Nah Nah, and her most personal name:

Q'Nah Nah Bi'eisha.

"Accept this offering of eighteen thousand Crackerish souls. Accept the hundred and eleven of my constituents, whose souls lie deep inside of Que, which I willingly sacrificed in the winter of 2020 – Cancun was lovely! Ol' Constructs, upon this sacrifice, count the old oaths fulfilled. Release Hugin. Release Munin. Release Sleipnir. Release all the remnants of Odin's power trapped within Que, the Earth, and whose bodily form rests upon her throne in Cancun – I know because I've been there! Ol' Constructs: recognize the seals of DeNagaer the White, who rules the sixteenth dungeon of the Confederacy, and the Magada Gaga, the Covfefe, who is the bent crown upon the seven elephants. Ol' Constructs, I command thee: answer my plea!"

Doom befell the House of Sardis, for the Texan's request was granted. Instantly, the soldiers' souls linked to Cody lost their allures – their appearances – and flashed like human silhouettes of blue, yellow, and then green. The souls moaned as their essences were like batteries, charging the pentagram upon Rupert's puggy stomach. And with great calamity, all eghteen thousand souls flashed like fractured bolts of green lightning and were consumed by the pentagram whole. Rupert fell to the jeweled floor upon his back in great agony, screaming Que's secret name, a secret no more. And as he laid there, limp like a bitch who had a Mitch stuck up his ass like a stick, Rupert knew that he had been played by the Magada. And he cursed his dealings with Q'Nah Nah Bi'eisha. In that moment, Rupert knew that he was a fool for he and the Republicans to think that Q'Nah could be controlled. After all, it was no secret that Q'Nah despised the likes of Rupert and his kind, who were climate deniers.

"Hot Alabama!" Rupert screamed in agony. "I never should

have followed the Magada, for all he knows is betrayal. I never should have listened to that blackish Q'Nah Nah Bi'eisha for all she knows in contempt for mankind who grows upon her like cancer. I never should have left my Redneck people. I never should have went to Cancun."

The elephants moved and bled upon the pentagram as they screamed out the names of the seven states marked by the Magada. Then, each elephant called upon the seven Satans – the first of the fallen angels – who each coveted a Confederate state. As each fallen angel was named, each of the Confederate states generated great spiritual power that reached across the veil and poured into Sardis. And the House of Sardis rocked to its roots and grew dim of its spectacular light.

Rupert's stomach bulged. The twisted beasts upon his fat began to crawl from the allure of his soul. The elephants bled black and red globs of blood as each wailed the name of a once-prosperous American state to which the Kingdom of Heaven would lay waste in the last days. As each elephant emerged and spoke, one after another blew its trunk and shook Sardis. The suffering beasts rose and made bellowing sounds that ached the ears of the angels adhered to their posts, the elephants merged into a gigantic black mass and took the allure of a red and green glowing fractured egg. And every angel in view was powerless to assist, for they all swore sacred oaths to duty and would never abandon their posts.

Act Thirteen

The Universe in the Rafters

"My brother, look at this pence!" the Archangel Keshawn said to the Archangel Duante. Fraternal brothers of the highest angelic order, the Archangels had been side by side since the dawn of the angels and were present at the birth of Cain, the Archangel Samuel's bastard son. And together, they had suffered greatly for the sake of man. They were among the few Archangels who lived through all of Heaven's wars, for most were wiped out by *Grimmoiril*, the Supreme Being who is Death, well before the first brick of Heaven was laid.

The Seraphs – angels with six wings – stood upon a soaring platform of stone and ore that sustained four large lazer cannons that circled the outermost rim of the universe within the rafters of Sardis. The micro-universe was taken from a humanoid who ascended to a Mormon godship named Tera Phim. Phim was an odd godling who lived, died, and ascended to godhood all before the AllGod's eyes. But, what made Tera Phim so bizarre was that he was the only godling who came from the AllGod's light first as a humanoid. I know it's strange, but as I was present at the time of Tera Phim, I'll share a bit of history concerning the Archangels Keshawn and Duante and how they came to guard that universe.

It was the third cycle of the second universe ever created by the AllGod, and for the first time, many godlings, such as the

Orishas and the Norsemen, poured out from his light. But, also was born Tera Phim, the first humanoid who had a spirit similar to a mortal's soul. As Tera Phim was the only one of his kind, his rapid ascension into Mormon godhood was assured, for he lived a short but profoundly spiritual life. And throughout his life, Phim naturally discovered and followed the Church's principles without prompting or awareness, for there was not another like him to sway him astray.

So, Phim, a brown-skinned, three-eyed, sprightly fellow short of stature and old of spirit, ascended and emerged a godling, as the intergalactic Mormon legend goes. His first act was to make himself fancy, and he cast himself a beautiful, flowing robe of yellow, black, and burgundy silks and diamonds upon his two lobes. Then, Phin projected a universe he created from his thoughts and wore the swirling creation upon his forehead like jewelry. He also manifested three godlings from his mind, and they were with him always. He worshiped the godlings as they represented all the desires he denied himself in his First Life. And so he made these godlings of money, lust, and purification and honored them at all times.

Well, the AllGod didn't like that shit – not at all. And you know how he gets down. So, almost as soon as the AllFather discovered Tera Phim's existence and the mockery of life that was his jewelry, the AllGod sent the Sky God, Lord Olorun, to dispatch all four of the godlings and destroy the universe in which Phim created.

As it was at the time, Lord Olorun, the Chief Orisha, was the AllGod's herald and the first to carry the Sword of Fire, the sword of the herald. As ordered, Lord Olorun destroyed Tera Phim and two of the godlings he projected. However, the Sky God, whose wisdom is admired by the AllGod, spared the godling Laquisha and the universe that Phin created. Olorun did not find Laquisha or the stars that Phin made offensive.

The Orisha and the goddess returned to the AllGod and prostrated before him. Olorun vouched for the godling and the microverse and asked for both to be spared. And so, the AllGod did, for he loved Olorun so.

And when this universe was formed, Laquisha, the Goddess of Purification, was allowed to follow the Sky God, Olorun, to Africa, the sacred home of the Orishas.

Laquisha was limited to its shores but roamed the continent wherever and as much as she liked. And the universe that Tera Phim constructed now sits in the rafters of Sardis. And it is the Archangels Keshawn and Duante who are its sworn protectors.

"Ha! The carlsontucking (motherfucking) pale apes are at it again," said Keshawn, who had long watched the proceedings of Sardis from his post. "Should we assist the Jew or Nah? If I don't have to, I won't." Keshawn laughed, for it was easier than crying. "I'd rather not risk another wing or the loss of more feathers over these half-breeds.

"During the first days under the tutelage of pain, I learned that unfortunate lesson – for real, for real."

Keshawn whipped his five wings and fanned the fumes of the Father Strain across the cosmos; the lowest wing upon his right was severed during the war over Cain. And, the attachments that Keshawn had remaining made the faintest whistle, for they had small pinholes where feathers used to belong and would catch the thinnest of airstreams each time the Seraph would flutter or set flight.

"Aye, Duante!" continued Keshawn as he reminisced about the dark era of the angels. "Do you remember how many angels died in the last war over these mischievous apes? Do you remember their names, huh, brother? I do. I also remember the Morning Star's last rant against them – against Cain – and I bite my lip, I tell you! I dare not say he spoke the truth but you know he tucking did. I mean, just look at this pence."

The Archangel Duante listened as he looked down upon the dark happenings of Sardis. He shook his head, inhaled the fumes, sighed, and then replied:

"I try to forget Lucifer and his Sparrow Brigade," Duante said. "I try to forget all the traitors as they were and only remember the Satans that they became. We are immortal, brother, and the collection of bad memories is overwhelming. I try to only remember the good times, for I despise the rest." After thinking for a moment, Duante smiled.

"I remember the apes, brother," Duante said as he rubbed his partial limb; he lost most of his left arm in the war against Lucifer. "I remember the apes from the time before man crawled from their bellies. Adam's mother's name was Xhosa, I believe.

"Those apes were funny and fearless, and she was kind. Beyond their natural defensive instincts, they were reasonable. I liked those apes. And no immortal who has met the race of mankind would ever accuse them of being as rational as apes."

Keshawn leaned upon one of the spiritual cannons and laughed.

"I find it insulting that mankind evolved from primates!" Duante continued. "It is disrespectful to the ape. These crazy things that our father has developed and stuffed with his own energy and fashioned as a soul are nothing but trouble- always and forever!

"But, please, brother," Duante said, "say no more about it. The AllGod will not hesitate to return over angelic disrespect, and I care not to see him as most of you carlsontuckers. Whenever the AllFather comes around, it's some pence, a big steaming pile of it, and the occasion always concerns those malignant things he covets and craves but will never truly love him back." Then Keshawn interjected:

"...But that homecoming for B.B. King was lit!" Keshawn replied as he danced and dabbed a bit.

"Nah, Nah!" Duante said with slight laughter. "That was legit, but that just proves my point: the good times are sliced thin like the last loaf." Duante threw back his tightly woven braids of hair from the front of his golden yet battered breast shield. With his gold and purple robe waving in the solar breeze, Duante walked to the platform's edge. He stared upon the distant proceedings of Sardis. He once again was torn over man. The smile upon his face slowly disappeared, and his right hand became firm upon his lance. He peered intensely at the Advocate, who he always felt hid things.

"Nevertheless," Duante said as he sighed, "the AllFather gave the Jew Warlord full authority over this place, and for all his shortcomings as a half-breed godling, you know as well as I that he is a master tactician. I would not tangle with him on my best day or with the greatest army. He is a peculiar immortal who has brought human cunning to the stratagem of Heaven. You never know what really is on his mind, and every truth he says is double talk – calamity upon calamity."

Keshawn lifted up his breastplate and reached inside his Allan Guth. He pulled out three zips of that Stardog and emptied them into the cauldron.

"Whewwww!" Keshawn said. "Now we flying, baby! Whewww!"

Keshawn fluttered his wings and hovered above the

platform, staying aligned with it as it soared. "Why is he not worried about the Ether? It's never down, which is strange enough, but he cannot return to Earth if needed without it, right? He travels through the Ether, the holy spirit, doesn't he?" Keshawn asked.

"That's a wise tale," Duante replied. "I've never seen him use it for teleportation or the AllGod. They have various forms of Alchemy for that type of mobility. No. No one travels the Ether except the AllSpirit and the spirits he has trapped in it. The Ether emits from the AllSpirit's Domain. And, if the Ether is corrupt, then that great golem of smoke must be aware of it.

"But, yes, the Advocate knows as well. He knows that no matter how much he smokes the God Bush or any other strain less potent, he can not spiritually connect to the Ether. And without it, we are blind and deaf in the spiritual realm.

"Brother, I believe the Jew to be a trickster at heart, just like the Earth's spirit, Q'Nah Nah. He's most definitely hiding something. Even when cut off from the Ether, which contains all the spiritual realm's real-time information, the Advocate does not flinch. He seems not to care.

"I would rather the Advocate smite the sassy pale face and move on. He gives two tucks about the significant disconnect of the Ether, but as soon as a 'Karen' presents herself, it is chaos in this carlsontucker! He stalls all his father's great works for the sake of a crazy Gaetz. But forget about it, Keshawn. It is his business. The Advocate manages Heaven according to his understanding of Mormon Law, and his interpretation is final. So, let those ruined Crackerish souls upon Sardis' floor be as the Forever War; his tucking problem."

"Aye! You are right!" Keshawn replied. He thought about Duante's words as he stared down at the cauldron of half-burned marijuana that smoked near his feet. Then, once again, Keshawn looked down upon the evil that erupted in Sardis and said:

"Yes! Let them destroy this tucking place as they have destroyed Q'Nah Nah, the first planet they were blessed with. And if this is what the trickster planet is doing, then I applaud her, and, I will not abandon my post to undo what she has done. Let's see how far the pale apes get this time."

Act Fourteen

The Egg the Republicans Laid

The Seraphim Keshawn and Duante starred down from the microverse and shook their heads at the coonery that the caucasians had crafted in the House of Sardis. The egg that the Texan, Rupert, had unwittingly given birth to with an ol' Bitch Ass Magic, the magic of White Phuckery, consumed him, and he was no more. But, what started as an unwitting, well-lubricated Texas man and eighteen thousand souls transformed into a horror unlike Heaven had ever seen. It was a spectacle that Rupert would have aborted if given a chance. However, it was magic that Q'Nah Nah had prescribed, and she made it so that it could not be undone. The spirit of Earth, who was Q'Nah Nah, despised anti-abortionists, who were like the cheerleaders of ticks and mites in her eyes, down to her molten core.

Behold! The egg rose high within the mist of Sardis and began to do wicked things. The egg glow turned black and its shadow was like light and it hardened, vibrated, and then sprouted four raven wings. Where the wings sprouted, the shell shattered and was sent flying across Sardis. Then the atrocity sprayed pointed icicles and snow out from the cracks where the wings unfolded, and thick clouds of smoke that carried curses in its breeze swirled all around the beast's remaining surface. When the broken shards of the shell shot across Sardis, they fired in all directions, impaling many souls and decapitating many others, and thus destroying them. With each scream, the beast paralyzed souls in its range so that none could escape. Then the beast ingulfed each soul that it paralyzed, feeding on the energy of its victims. And five hundred angels positioned in advance of Sardis, outside Heaven but still near its gardens, listened helplessly as the egg-shaped mass went through its seasons, for they could not abandon their appointed positions.

The beast's wings were so massive that the creature created incredible wind storms of snow and ice inside Sardis and blew many souls right out of the building and into the open space before the gardens. Some souls were engulfed by the creature's smoke and were cursed, and their souls were frozen where they stood. Tens of thousands of souls ran screaming past the gardens where the musicians gathered, and the angels stood their posts. The musicians, many of whom were rappers peacefully awaiting the Advocate to 'loophole' their judgments, ran screaming along with the souls from Sardis, although not knowing why they were running in the first place. And the angels, many of varying class, remained still and solemn in their oaths, for they would not sacrifice their place in the AllGod's eyes for the sake of the Kingdom of Heaven. A Kingdom that no angel felt was his home.

The Redneck Books of Life, who had come to Sardis with the ability to spew shit from their mouths, returned from what seemed like every shadow or crevice within Sardis that existed. Six hundred of the talking books circled the winged beast and its remaining shell and formed a massive ring, glowing red and emitting flames that burst and erupted like a furnace.

The Advocate, who was still in Sardis conducting his Dark Alchemy, turned to speak to D'jon, who had white-knuckled the door of E.1999. D'jon was glued to the entrance of the Pavilion, intensely watching the Balboa tree, anticipating its holy acts. And although the great Hall is massive, as it is a quantum zone that warps in height, width, and length, the Advocate spoke to D'jon as if he was standing within earshot.

"D'jon Hardgrove, D'jon the Faithful, D'jon, Mister bend the corner on two wheels while never spilling the Marlow," the Advocate said, "I knew you every day of your life as you've always prayed and thought of me. You called my name and my father's name in every moment – the good, not just the bad. And besides…"

D'jon, who manifested in Heaven in his bus driver's uniform as he loved the job due to all the Gaetz (ass) that bounced down the bus path regularly, was startled by the AllProphet and whipped his head toward the Advocate. He puckered his face like a giant butt hole that was suddenly surprised.

"You can't sing to save your soul!" the AllProphet said and laughed. D'jon screwed his face, but he let his people slide.

"You have earned your place in Heaven," the Advocate continued. "D'jon, I am pressed firmly between stagnation, hostility, and my father's agenda. So quickly, come back to the defendant's table, step over Sara, who seems to be our long-term resident Karen, and make your way to the Grand Door, labeled 22, and into Paradise."

Soon after he spoke, the Advocate drew his breath in deep and stumbled a bit. He was exhausted. The cast of Dark Alchemy just performed was complete; however, the strain of that great work temporarily drained his soul. Nevertheless, the result was accomplished. The Baobab Tree firmly took root in the Pavilion and was ready to shed its fruit for those wafering caretakers. The second stream of his mighty cast, the Methuselah Root, reached the gardens of Addisu's Offspring and struck the mana deep, shaking the battalion of angels that stood before its botanicals.

The angels were yet to witness the running and scattering of the souls from Sardis. But the third stream of the Advocate's mighty cast traveled amongst the clouds of the astral plane as if it was a flock of doves and set root in a valley, far from the Kingdom's gates.

"No!" squealed Sara. "You mean room 222!" Like most Karens, Sara could not resist inserting herself into a situation. But, in her defense, she had good authority. A box containing the complete Rick Ross discography sits in the corner of a Port of Saint Joe's apartment, owned by Sara's son, who inherited the CDs upon her demise. Sara loved the Biggest Boss, a Floridian to his heart. And Sara was very proud that she had purchased each album and single release with her own money, resisting the lifelong urge to boost.

"That's room 222!" Sara repeated.

"No, Karen! I mean, Amber! I mean Sara – pence!" Musa said frantically as he fumbled to explain. "So sorry," Musa said, embarrassed to have spent so much time with the bubble-bodied soul, not to have gotten her name right. In his defense, she was irritating as fuck, as all Karens are. Musa continued.

"'No, Sara,' is what I meant to say – No, Sara!" reaffirmed Governor Musa. "Number 22! That's Door Number 22." Then D'jon looked up and said:

"Oh! I know them birds go for 22!" D'jon replied. He had noticed many flocks of various birds of air and ground would enter and exit the Grand Door, as it would appear whenever they migrated through the Kingdom.

"Yes, D'jon," the Advocate replied, "the birds do indeed flock to Door Number 22. It serves as one of the main access into Heaven and all manner of fowl – except ravens and crows – are free to go into these places of mysteries as they please. But it is just a short walk for you, my son. No flight or migration necessary." D'jon laughed for a moment. But as he chuckled a bit, he happened to look up and saw three Pterodactyl chase a flock of Yi across the vast ceiling which the birds considered sky. With his left hand still gripped upon the Pavilion's door, D'jon shook his head, for he was consistently amazed and pleased by everything he witnessed in the House of Sardis.

"Pence!" D'jon replied with lamentation in his voice. "Cuz, I don't know. I mean, this place is crazy! And I feel all this negative energy, you know? It's the way one would feel when too many Wafers tightly congregate together like thick batter – it's a recipe for disaster. Maybe it isn't just these Level One Crackers you are about to thrash. You've never before used your Dark Alchemy for something so small and I've been here for at least a hundred years. Perhaps you cast it because of the abundant Rednecks that stir in this place. I have seen many of them running around here in unusual fashion. And where is that lowly politician from Texas, just before me? I do not like that pencytucker at all." D'jon grew anxious.

"D'jon," the Advocate exclaimed, "I will encourage you just as I have encouraged all who fear the Second Life, my son: don't tuck up on me now!" D'jon stiffened up as he continued watching the events of Sardis. The Advocate then touched his left thumb to the pentagram-engraved coin upon the adjoining palm and ignited the Dark Alchemy cast: Ten Toes Deep. The Advocate sunk into the spiraling transmutation portal of green light that appeared beneath him, only to rise from another outlet upon the jeweled floor, positioned next to D'jon. Musa quickly walked over to D'jon and the Advocate, stepping over Sara in the process. The Advocate continued.

"I have no time to fully explain the complexity of what

you've seen since you've been here nor what you think is the simplicity of Heaven. Go back toward the light of judgment which lies there between the Kings and all the court's heavenly host." Then the AllProphet whispered in Sara's Direction so that she could hear his discontent. "The Grand Door, which is, by the way, Sara, numbered 22, is accessible, for you are permitted to enter by my word."

Then the Advocate turned his fiery eyes toward the door. D'jon's eyes followed. He gazed upon the door as the magnificent light of Heaven burst through its seams, light much brighter than Sardis, the Pavilion, or the sky that covered the House of Sardis.

"The light of Heaven," D'jon said, astounded, "it is truly magnificent!" He rolled his shoulders back and stood proudly. "I never get tired of watching souls walk through that door. Hearing the choir sing and the Kings celebrate. Truth be told, it's the main reason I have never pressed you about being here. There is no tale that's been told with a happier ending. But, the vibe seems ill here and completely out of order. Now, that it is upon me – the gift of eternal life – I might have fallen in love with the promise more than the actual reward. Big Homie, I have enjoyed my time here. I think being absent from your presence would be too much for me to bear."

"D'jon, I urge you to reconsider," the Advocate exclaimed as they gazed at the Grand Door in the distance, mesmerized by the beams of light that burst from its seams. "This is not an occasion for sadness or fear. No, D'jon. This is nothing but a joyous moment, ill vibes aside. Do not forsake Paradise for the sake of our friendship. If I was allowed within the Kingdom's walls, I would Josh Hawley (a dick running hysterically) my way through that door, giving two tucks about Sardis, for salvation is up to each and every soul. But, I cannot. for my father declared long ago that I may not enter the Kingdom's main body until I fulfill my oath to establish his Kingdom on Earth; a true earthly paradise. But, you, D'jon, you may have the spiritual Paradise – right here and now! So, I will encourage you to do as your AllSavior did back in the day: bear the cross and save yourself! Now turn that other cheek and roll out, for the act of a soul to deny Heaven is ludicrous!

"Do not run toward oblivion, D'jon, but turn away. If you stay in Sardis, you risk not only your Second Life but your chance to enter the Kingdom entirely. Soon doom will befall this great Hall of Heaven. A similac storm (a mob of spoiled, frustrated Whites) has formed against me, once again, and it now blows heavily upon Heaven's outer gates. Many souls will perish here. But fear not. The power of the Kingdom is as mighty as its ruler. The strength of the Kingdom is everlasting. So, be reassured, D'jon, for this is not the fighting season of Revelations, but a small skirmish that I have allowed to occur. Heaven's warriors eagerly await the opportunity to show the enemy a portion of the vigor that the Confederacy will face in the final days. It is exactly as the Book of Drake suggests: the challenge before us is oppy at best."

"Ooh, pence!" D'jon said as he dipped his shoulder like a gangsta. "AllProphet, that's that knife talk! Ehh mane, Ninth Born, you cunning nigga, what is this sinister business you allude to? Similacs? White phuckery I think you allude to." The Advocate blushed and laughed in reply, for he loved being called the enduring term "nigga." Hearing it made him feel down, which is up for you principled Crackers. Nevertheless, D'jon stared. But, just as he had begun to press the Advocate with inquiry, the soul of the burly bus driver saw the Grand Door open just a sliver before the throne. Still, he was torn between walking into Heaven as an official citizen and leaving the Halfbred Jew he called friend amid ill vibes or bearing witness to the acts of the Baobab tree, which he hoped would be something gnarly and would smite the Crackers' server.

"Do you guys hear screaming?" Sara whimpered from the floor. "I hear other White women screaming hysterically in the distance. I regrettably admit, we 'Karens' can sense when one of us is distressed. Does anyone else hear MItches (bitches) losing their mind?"

"That depends, Sara," the Advocate said from over his shoulder, "will you continue to lay upon the floor?" Sara curled up into a tighter ball upon the floor and continued whimpering.

"Then no," the Advocate said. "Until you lift yourself from the floor, it is not your concern – stand up, woman."

Suddenly, from the center of the Hall rushed the screams of many terrified souls, crying out for salvation, praying for escape from the wretched beast that grew in size and fury with every soul it consumed. The cries of the fearful were like the roar of tidal waves crashing down upon the calmness of the court and the posture of the Kings and angels. Many of the angels within the legions that guarded the Grand Door grew weary as the chaos grew closer. Then, like a herd of stampeding steers, millions of the unjudged bombarded the court proceedings. The frantic souls scurried atop one another, fruitlessly banging and clambering at every door that stood on the right side of Sardis. Many of them behaved as they did in the First Life and dashed through the fog toward the Throne of Judgment in hopes of finding the Advocate at his appointed station. However, he was still with D'jon making their way back toward the Grand Door.

But, in all the chaos and the madness that had overtaken

many of them, no soul dared pass the pathway that led to the Grand Door. The angels stationed beyond that threshold presented just as much danger as the beast. As soon as the mayhem broke out, the angelic legions went from a position of attention to one of attack. The angels drew their swords and clanked them upon their shields, chanting an anthem of modern days that they had taken as their own in defiance of the threat of men. Amidst the mayhem, an angel who was the old Gunnery Sergeant of the Bone Crushers sang out and all the angels from both legions answered back:

Ol' Gunny:

"Ye' AllFather who has long been gone from Heaven.

"Your wayward children think we playin', think we half steppin'.

"Oh' legions of the Lord, before the throne, please won't you tell 'em?"

Angelic Legions:

"We ready! We ready! The Kingdom of the Lord is never ever scared!"

Amidst the mayhem, the Demonic Counsel reveled in the chaos, for it was the destruction of Heaven that every angel cast from Paradise hoped for. But still, the destruction of Heaven at the hands of the Cracker Nation and not Hell was a bitter pill to swallow for the demons. So, Belial donned what was left of his angelic armor that had seen its day after the fall, weathered armor covered in a thin brimstone salt.

"DeNagaer," Belial said. "Donn your like cowboy hat and ensemble. I believe I shall have you ride upon Rudy's shoulder. We shall lasso in and wrangle to Hell as many of the corrupted souls here in Sardis as we can, including those who oppose Heaven. We shall punish these Crackers who assault Heaven in

Odin or the Magada's name and not in the name of the Devil or the Confederacy who they should truly serve."

"These pencetucking carlsontuckers are an evil all to their own," Rudy replied. "This pence horde of insurrectionists whose books claim lineage from the First Fallen, shall rue the day that the Cracker Nation thought themselves better than Hell, the master they serve. We shall have our day, but it shall not be here at Heaven's gate. Come, DeNagaer, you were always lost without the guidance of Hell."

"I'm sorry, Holy Roller," D'jon said as the souls, who were like wild prey, pushed through the fog and past the Advocate in hopes of finding sanctuary in E.1999 or another of Heaven's Pavilion. They did not.

"I would never forsake you for the sake of myself," D'jon said. "You died for me, Big Homie. I cannot, in good conscience, leave you to face this Gaetz-like calamity all by your lonely. That sort of weakness, nay, selfishness is not gangster and you already know what I am all about."

"That 'G' pence!" The Advocate replied with renewed vigor. "That righteous hustle in the midst of a resistant struggle."

"Yeah-yeah!" D'jon said. "But, what of the carlsontucking lion?" D'jon asked the Advocate, sticking out his chest and smiling for he knew the Advocate's heart. The Advocate replied:

"But, lions roar and fear no rumble!" the Advocate bolstered.

"Alabama tucking yeah!" D'jon said. "And my spirit is like Elisha's. Give me a double serving of whatever befalls you cause I got your back Big Homie. Especially if the legions will not break their ranks before the door, disregarding their purpose and duty, despite the presence of great evil." Then, the AllProphet stopped dead in his tracks and looked upon D'jon, whose face was eager like a player on the third string, warming a cold hard bench. The Advocate turned to D'jon, mere yards from the Grand Door, and said:

"All right, D'jon!" the Advocate replied in amusement. "In for a pound are we?

"Well, I can contend with godlings, demi-gods, and any of the Satans. I can even contend with the evil in the heart of almost every man, but I am no match for you, D'jon. You've wrestled with the AllSavior and have won."

So, D'jon and the Advocate walked to the front of Sardis and positioned themselves in front of the corridor that led to the Grand Door, just before the threshold that separated the Thirty-Sixth Chamber and the court. Sara, still upon the floor, had crawled before the Advocate's table and continued to cry like a chirping bird. It was there at that moment that the Advocate, the AllSavior, covered D'jon in sparkling silver and gold armor, making him a spiritual warrior of Heaven. Then the Advocate placed D'jon in his personal guard, who were all immortal Christian souls. And the Advocate smiled as the Kings behind him smiled, for they were all ready for war upon the Cracker Nation's next move.

TO BE CONTINUED

Song Collective

Don't You Care
Beat BPM 118 https://youtu.be/7AJ_THgnJ8g)

(Intro – Larry: 00:02)
"Ooh God, don't you care? Ooh God, do you even... care? Ooh God, please don't...
"Forsake us, don't you dare."
(1st Chorus – Officer Token: 00:16)
"Ohh, Ohh, It's never fair.
"Ooh-Ooh, It's never even... fair.
"Ooh God – please don't forsake the pales. Ooh, God, don't you care?"

(2nd Chorus – White Mob: 00:32)
"Ooh God, don't you care?
"We, the blue eyes and blonde-haired?
"Ooh God, please admit we're 'very special?' Ooh God, make it fair."

(Verse 1- Larry: 00:48)
"My daddy loved Christ.
"Love the idea of a White Paradise. Devoted his whole life,
"To livin' right, every day, he prayed twice.
(00:56)
"And every single night,
"He would thank God for being just the right type of White, "That

Mmm-mmm, Sandra Bullock type of creamy white.
"Ooooh, that sounds nice. (01:04)
"He hated nobody;
"He just loved being White,
"I ask: what's wrong with that?
"Why are White men's souls forever subjugated to the Lord's
"wrath?
(01:12)
"This is making no sense. There's no forgiving this pence (bitch),
Harassing our good Lord and Savior and pence (shit)?
"Why is he so cool with it?
"Why was my daddy not acquitted? – Hell nah!"